WOMEN WRITERS
AND THE GREAT WAR

TWAYNE'S

LITERATURE
&
SOCIETY

SERIES

WOMEN WRITERS AND THE GREAT WAR

Dorothy Goldman
With Jane Gledhill and Judith Hattaway

Twayne Publishers
AN IMPRINT OF SIMON & SCHUSTER MACMILLAN
NEW YORK

PRENTICE HALL INTERNATIONAL
LONDON • MEXICO CITY • NEW DELHI • SINGAPORE • SYDNEY • TORONTO

Twayne's Literature & Society Series No. 7

Women Writers and the Great War

Dorothy Goldman with Jane Gledhill and Judith Hattaway

Copyright © 1995 by Twayne Publishers

Twayne Publishers
An Imprint of Simon & Schuster Macmillan
866 Third Avenue
New York, New York 10022

Library of Congress Cataloging-in-Publication Data

Goldman, Dorothy.
    Women writers and the Great War / Dorothy Goldman with Jane Gledhill and Judith Hattaway.
        p.   cm.—(Twayne's literature & society series: TLS 7)
    Includes bibliographical references and index.
    ISBN 0-8057-8858-1
    1. English literature—Women authors—History and criticism.   2. World War, 1914–1918—Great Britain—Literature and the war.   3. World War, 1914–1918—United States—Literature and the war.   4. American literature—Women authors—History and criticism.   5. American literature—20th century—History and criticism.   6. English literature—20th century—History and criticism.   7. Women and literature—History—20th century.   8. World War, 1914–1918— Women.   I. Gledhill, Jane.   II. Hattaway, Judith.   III. Title.   IV. Series: Twayne's literature & society series: no. 7.
PR478.W65G65   1995
820.9′358′0904—dc20

94-24561
CIP

The paper used in this publication meets the minimum requirements of American National Standard for Information Sciences—Permanence of Paper for Printed Library Materials, ANSI Z39.48-1984. ⊗™

10 9 8 7 6 5 4 3 2 1

Printed in the United States of America

CONTENTS

ACKNOWLEDGMENTS

Grateful acknowledgment is made to the publishers and individuals listed below for permission to reprint from the following works:

Behind the Lines: Gender and the Two World Wars, edited by Margaret Randolph Higonnet, Jane Jenson, Sonya Michel, and Margaret Collins Weitz (New Haven and London: Yale University Press, 1987). Copyright © 1987 by Margaret Randolph Higonnet. Reprinted by permission of Yale University Press.

The Great War and Women's Consciousness: Images of Militarism and Womanhood in Women's Writings, 1914–1964 by Claire M. Tylee (London: Macmillan, 1990; Iowa City: University of Iowa Press, 1990). Copyright © 1990 by Claire M. Tylee. Reprinted by permission of Macmillan and University of Iowa Press.

Dorothy Littlejohn, unpublished manuscript, Imperial War Museum Archives. Reprinted by permission of Rachel A. Hedderwick.

Excerpts from *Mrs. Dalloway* by Virginia Woolf (London: Hogarth Press, 1925). Copyright © 1925 by Harcourt Brace & Company and renewed 1953 by Leonard Woolf. Reprinted by permission of Harcourt Brace & Company

PREFACE

[Writing about war conveys experiences that] involved the whole self—of that time in the writer's life when he was most sharply alive.
—Storm Jameson, *No Time Like the Present*

We have to face our war.
—Katherine Mansfield

THROUGHOUT HISTORY WAR HAS TAKEN A HEAVIER PHYSICAL toll on men than women. Despite the burdens it has imposed on civilian populations, the brunt of injury, mutilation, and death has been borne by men. It is not our intention to detract from that fact. This book, however, takes as its central premise the significance of World War I to women.

World War I introduced soldiers to the horrors that came to define modern warfare—barbed wire, trench warfare, gas, the bayonet, the tank, and the airplane. Despite that, and the fact that in cultural terms, in terms of literary history and the canon of war writing, the Great War was a man's war, the focus of our attention will be on how women writers realized their war. Although the very phrase "the war poets" has entered the language to designate both the nature of the soldiers in this war and the writing in which they captured their experiences, we will concentrate on women's literary achievements.

For women, too, the war brought radical and unexpected experiences— loss, bereavement, war work, travel, a change in sexual mores—all of which coincided with, and affected, the continuing struggle for the vote, changing employment patterns, and experimental art forms. The need to capture some- thing of the experience of those years was clearly felt as desperately by women as by men.

The forms their writing took are many. Mothers, sisters, wives, lovers— all became letter writers, and many kept diaries. Their unpublished writings in the Archives of the Imperial War Museum in London have a particular immediacy and poignancy. The published works are richly varied. There are poems, many of which originally appeared in literary magazines, and short stories, with the patriotic ones often published in women's magazines. The novels range from those which present simple jingoistic attitudes and espouse traditional pieties, through those which express confusion and distress, to those which present clear perceptions and analyses. Informal diaries docu- ment work on the home front, escapes from occupied Europe, and nursing. Collections of journalism express patriotic or suffragist sentiment, report on visits to France, and seek support for war charities. Memoirs recall women's experiences as nurses, doctors, and other volunteers at the war front, or serve as memorials to the loved and lost. These writings vary in form, in aesthetic value, and in attitude, explicit and implicit; but each is marked by a sense that something was happening in these years that needed recording and analyzing.

Yet what women wrote about this period has been largely forgotten, or granted only grudging recognition, and its vision has been submerged under masculine myths about the war and war literature. This book does not attempt to make cultural, social, or political judgments on the period, and it only does so when it is necessary to extrapolate a literary point. During the last decade or so, feminist critics have confronted these issues in all their complexity; any disagreement we may have with their emphases or conclusions is over- shadowed by our gratitude for their recognition of the subject and their establishment of its central position in any understanding of twentieth- century women's writing. We focus instead on reassessing the literature women produced and asking how the patterns that emerge from the reassess- ment can contribute to our understanding of this outpouring. Implicit throughout the book is a comparison with what men wrote about the war.

The study begins with "The War and Women," a tripartite examination of the war. To enable those unfamiliar with the history of the war to understand references to seminal and symbolic events and terms, a simple narrative, told mainly from the English point of view, attempts to establish the sequence of important battles, the methods of warfare, the military strategy, the geographical positions of the opposing sides; where appropriate—as in the case of recruitment, trench warfare, pacifism, treatment of the wounded—the position of women vis-à-vis men's experience is touched on. The second section, which provides factual information about women's experiences during the war, highlights the paradoxes created by their involvement in the war: the conflict between war work and pacifism; the effect of the war on the struggles for emancipation and suffrage; women's wartime civilian employment, postwar reversion to domesticity, and developing political consciousness; the issues raised by their acceptance of military discipline in volunteer and national organizations; the uncertain and unstable relationship between women's knowledge of the war and their options for expression. This opening chapter concludes with the private voices of some of the women writers themselves, in diaries and memoirs not intended for publication. Before addressing the literary issues raised by the means that women found to make their voice public, there is a selection of informal writings from the period by women that describe their experience of their war and the reflection of men's experience of theirs.

The second chapter, "The Dilemma of Subject," seeks to discover if *what* women wrote about provides a common or communal agenda. In this context the cultural priority allocated to men's firsthand descriptions of battle is examined as a possible cause of the neglect, even rejection, of women's writing, and the writings by women about battle—understandably limited in number as they are—are assessed. An analysis of the most common subjects of women's writing (domestic affairs—in particular childbirth and the care of children; nursing, nurture, order) and the common metaphors in the manner of their expression uncovers a second shadowy list of concerns that appears to be gender-specific. But a close study of literary structure of women's narratives, their literary assumption of men's roles (as soldiers, casualties), and of the subjects common to men's and women's writing strengthens the argument that women's writing shares a deep internal structure with men's. The subjects women wrote about are also examined to discover those areas which are specific to women (the rejection of the familial role and the freedom war brought for some, for example). The chapter closes with a consideration of how far these subjects and the issues they comprehend define the question of sexual identity as being central to women's concerns.

Chapter 3, "Genre and Appropriated Form," extends the discussion to the use women made of particular genres and the extent to which they were able to expand and adapt them. In particular it takes as its subject the romance, which, it is argued, has a special resonance and function at transitional historical moments. The quest, a basic romance motif, offered writers a narrative framework, whether it took the form of an excursion into danger or into cynical disillusion. Women writers' mediation between the attempt to embrace the traditional form and the need to find a new mode for expression is examined, in particular in works by Dorothy Stanley, Cicely Hamilton, May Sinclair, Enid Bagnold, Evadne Price, and Katherine Mansfield. Search, fantasy, enchantment, liberation, enlightenment, revelation, transformation, individualism: these are the concepts that were put to use in writing during and after the war by men and women. The strain that the birth of new variants put on the romance and the resultant difficulty of ends and closures is examined to unravel another strand of literary response—one both men and women shared.

In the light of the connections between men's and women's war writing established in chapters 2 and 3, chapter 4, "Canon and Tradition," attempts to explain where women's writing fits—or, more accurately, has been considered not to fit—into the literary history of the period. Initially through an examination of different vocabularies employed at the time, the chapter argues that women writers, like men, simultaneously used a referential style to realize a traditional attitude toward the war and, as illustrated by Mary Borden, a modernist approach of fragmentation to realize an inexplicable experience of confusion and pain. This double approach, which locates the origin of modernism in the prewar avant-garde movements, is preferred to the simpler belief that it was the experience of the war that forced the new idiom into existence. Necessarily, therefore, women are found to owe as great a debt, and to offer as great a contribution, to modernism as their male counterparts. The literary means required to convey the dehumanization and psychic wounds caused by the war—the inward state of wounded consciousness—are examined and found to have been significant for, and profoundly developed by, women writers; Rose Macaulay and Virginia Woolf, in particular, are examined in this context. The traditional strengths of women's writing (detail, internalization, domestic- and personal-referencing, the dissection of the apparently trivial and social, indirection), which contributed to their characteristic ability to make real the inner and the vulnerable, appear to encourage their exclusion from the canon. Further reasons for the neglect of the contribution of women war writers to the development of modernism are rehearsed, including the mythologizing of the exclusivity of men's wartime experience.

Chapter 5, "A Change of Voice," considers how far it is possible to identify a common voice in women writers of the war years. Their experiences and attitudes were so various that any common identity will be underlying, rather than immediately apparent. An examination of the role of the war as a stimulus to writing leads to a consideration of the roles and the identities the war allowed women to adopt publicly, and the central importance of participation is suggested. As their perception of themselves as participants in public life and historical events grew, women began to experience what has been thought to be men's exclusive right to speak of the war. A belief in the authenticity and validity of their experience led them to the confident belief that they were authorized to narrate no less than their male counterparts. This tone is recognizable—even when what they narrate is confusion, incomprehension, nothing more than a tentative move toward understanding. Yet set alongside this need for and belief in their narrative role lay a profound respect and pity for what men were enduring, to which was allied the understanding that they were excluded from the soldiers' war and from the narration of that war. The chapter thus identifies the common note of the female voice as the need to write as both actor and spectator, this in turn requiring the resources of a conflated form that relies on both fiction and documentary.

Throughout the book we have adopted methodological approaches that have grown from our underlying beliefs. Our critical stance was formed at the outset by a profound respect for the method and scholarship of Paul Fussell. We have attempted to combine this with a critical recognition of the more overt feminist claims of such writers as Sandra Gilbert and with cognizance of the social and cultural concerns of such writers as Nicola Beauman and Jean Elshtain and the eclectic and illustrative approach of Claire Tylee.

To understand how women encoded the impact of an event of the magnitude of the war we have felt it necessary to range as widely as possible. We have not restricted our range of reference in terms of authorial perception or attitude (jingoist or pacifist, suffragist or angel of the house), and neither have we limited it to only English or American authors, to books written during the war years, or to writers who took an active or a passive role in the war. Our study includes the little-known author as well as unpublished material, and it is not our intention to offer exclusive analysis or interpretation of individual authors. By establishing literary concepts and queries as the focus of each chapter (subject, genre, canon, voice) we have been able to discuss individual authors in a cumulative manner—analyses of *Jacob's Room*, *Mrs. Dalloway*, and *To the Lighthouse* occur severally rather than sequentially, for example. This approach has enabled us constantly to place writers in the context of their peers. Widely respected authors (Rebecca West, Virginia Woolf, Radclyffe Hall, Willa Cather, Edith Wharton, Vera Brittain, Katherine Mansfield, and Gertrude Stein) are put alongside the merely respectable (Mildred Aldrich, E. M. Delafield, Dorothy Canfield, Gertrude Atherton, Mary Borden, Elizabeth von Arnim, Evadne Price, Rose Macaulay, Cicely Hamilton, and Enid Bagnold, for example), the inferior but interesting (such as Mary Roberts Rinehart, Olive Dent, Mrs. Humphry Ward, and Flora Sandes), and the now forgotten (Mabel Daggett, Else Janis, Josephine Therese, Grace S. Richmond, Meriel Buchanan, Mary Agnes Hamilton, Temple Bailey, and Dorothy Stanley). In all cases it is the underlying and connective tissue of literary context we have sought to examine.

The emphasis on breadth of reference and precise textual analysis and the reliance on supportive evidence from little-known authors have necessitated frequent and occasionally lengthy quotations. This has permitted us both precise literary analysis and generalization of wider patterns of response. The wider analysis we offer will be found to rest almost without exception on textual reference and quotation. Two restrictions only were felt to be necessary: we have dealt only with prose, and then only with prose written in English. The reasons for this relate directly to the aims of this examination. We felt that the structure of poetry, the density of its language, and the complexity of its organization made demands that would inhibit the inherently comparable assessments we wished to make; equally, the nature of the constraints to linguistic analysis imposed by translation were felt to be too strong to allow the inclusion of writers from, say, France and Germany.

We have responsibility for individual chapters—Jane Gledhill for chapter 1, Dorothy Goldman for the preface, chapters 2, 4, 5, and 6, and Judith Hattaway for chapter 3—but during the writing of this book we have each influenced the others' thoughts, opinions, critical attitudes, writing patterns, working lives, domestic concerns.

The women writers of the Great War were conscious of one another's work: "we did make a detour beyond Charley to pass round the Chateau de Villiers-sur-Marne,—the home of Francis Wilson's daughter, Madame Huard, and the scene of 'My Home on the Field of Honour,' " wrote Mildred Aldrich. "There, finding the big gates standing wide open, and only a few soldiers in the neglected park, we took the liberty of making the wide circular-drie part of our route, just to say we had been there, passing in front of the closed chateau."[1] And they were proud of one another: one American woman wrote of Aldrich's book, "Thank you for 'The Hill-Top on the Marne.' It is a good experience, spiritedly sketched, and I like the lady's pluck."[2] And Gertrude Stein said of Aldrich, "no one else had done as much propaganda for France as she had by her books which everyone in America read."[3] Edith Wharton reserves some of her highest praise for women as evidenced in this passage about Baroness T'Serclaes and Mairi Chisholm: "In one of those villas for nearly a year, two hearts at the highest pitch of human constancy have held up a light to the world. It is impossible to pass that house without a sense of awe. Because of the light that comes from it dead faiths have come to light, weak convictions have grown strong, fiery impulses have turned to long endurance, and long endurance has kept the fire of impulse."[4] We would like to feel that we have helped to rescue from neglect an important cultural moment in women's lives; that we have added to the understanding of literary functions; and that we have allowed some women to speak again through us to their granddaughters. It is to the women who lived through those years and attempted to speak to their peers and their descendants that we dedicate this book.

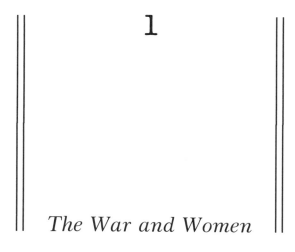

1

The War and Women

There are some things better left undescribed . . . perhaps in the afterwards, when time has somewhat deadened matters, you will hear of them.

—J. Hendrie, *Letters of a Durisdeer Soldier*

I sometimes wish it wasn't the English war convention to keep up this eternally frivolous manner. I so often want to say to a man straight out: "I think you are simply splendid to keep smiling like that when you are plunging back into all this horror which you loathe. Your courage and your gaiety make me ashamed of my own qualities which are never called upon to face one hundredth of what you go through. You dear smiling wonderful thing, all the wishes of my heart go with you"—or words to that effect! But one must never say them—it wouldn't do—it isn't done.

—Irene Rathbone, unpublished diary

THE FAMOUS WORDS OF SIR EDWARD GREY, THE BRITISH Foreign Secretary, as he faced the prospect of war were prophetic: "The lamps are going out all over Europe. We shall not see them lit again in our time."[1] A gauge of the extent to which the Great War has affected the cultural history of the twentieth century can be found in the extent to which it has changed our perception of light, landscape, and sky. Paul Fussell enlarges on this theme, explaining that during World War I soldiers used to dread daybreak, when fighting resumed, and that the sky was never blue but black, purple, and orange with smoke, gunfire, and flames.[2] Today we remain in awe of the bravery of those soldiers, and we still associate it with the twilight hour: "At the going down of the sun and in the morning / We will remember them."[3] Poppies still bloom in the fields of northern France and the neat, relentless rows of white crosses in Allied military cemeteries mark the grave-less dead whose lives sank into the mud of the western front.

It is significant that in two of the most interesting accounts of the war (by Keith Robbins and Marc Ferro[4]) the contributions made by women oc-cupy, respectively, two and one pages. To draw attention to this omission is not to make a case for "herstory" but rather to establish the necessity of illustrating and explaining the contribution women made during World War I. The point of departure taken by this study is that women had similar views to men about the war and that this is reflected in their commitment, their work, and their writing. Women sent men to the front and then re-ceived back their dead and wrote their epitaphs; they watched the sun set on English manhood.

With the German violation of Belgian neutrality, the events of 1914 moved irrevocably toward war. Sir Edward Grey wrote: "I was myself stirred with resentment at . . . Germany's crime and all I knew of Prussian militarism was hateful. But these must not be our motives for going to war. . . . The real reason [is] that if we didn't stand by France and stand up for Belgium against this aggression we should be isolated, discredited and hated."[5] Beth-mann-Hollweg, the German chancellor, was angered by Grey's attitude and that of the British people. "The steps taken by His Majesty's Government," he said, "were terrible to a degree just for one word, 'neutrality,' a word in wartime so often disregarded. Just for a scrap of paper Great Britain was going to make war on a kindred nation who desired nothing but friendship."[6] Thus, at the time of the war's outbreak, both nations held each other responsi-ble for whatever horrors might come in its train. There was to be no turning back.

On August Bank Holiday in 1914 crowds outside Buckingham Palace shouted "We want war." The beliefs of many pacifists in England, France, and Germany were subsumed in the belief that each country was fighting in self-defense. When war was declared on 4 August the commonly held view was that it would be over by Christmas. No one dreamed that trench warfare would develop and become a way of life, and of death, for four years and three months. No one realized that the war that broke out that summer would soon be called a world war. Though the action was concentrated in

France and Belgium, it would be a war that was fought in Central and East Africa, in Serbia, Russia, Egypt, Austria, and Gallipoli; the first British shot of the war was fired on the East African Coast.

The early invasion of France and Belgium by German troops on 3 August 1914 established a pattern of offensive and counteroffensive attacks. The protection of Belgium was the pretext for going to war, and its defense the first strategic imperative. In the early months of the war the concern of the Allies was to halt the German advance and prevent the German forces from reaching Paris. This was achieved, but at the expense of half a million casualties on both sides. As though to parody the belief that they were all acting in self-defense, it was a feature of the war that whenever one side planned and executed an offensive action it sustained the heaviest losses and that powers acting in self-defense had fewer casualties. This led to a reactive approach to warfare, which at the very outset reinforced the entrenchment that would become its defining characteristic.

The stationing of German forces as close as 50 miles from Paris resulted in the Battle of the Marne, 6–9 September 1914. Immediately, it became apparent that this war would not conform to heroic stereotypes. This was not battle as it had traditionally been understood: there were no sudden advances, no defined battleground, no decisive victories, only the capturing and losing of a few hundred yards of ground, at most a few miles of front, while behind the lines of barbed wire the trenches became deeper and more impenetrable, the mud thicker, and the stench of death and decomposition stronger.

By the end of 1914 there was deadlock on the western front. The Germans held their line, which ran from the Swiss frontier northward through the Vosges and the Meuse and up to Armentieres; facing them were the French. The Belgians held the tiny area around La Panne, and the British held the Somme to Bethune. Severe losses necessitated further recruitment both for the army and for nursing and auxiliary staff. On 11 October the recruiting bodies in England were accepting men who were at least five feet, five inches, in height; as early as 5 November, and after 30,000 casualties, a height of only five feet, three inches, was acceptable.

Meanwhile, the women at home were given daily encouragement to boost recruitment by advertisements like this:

TO THE YOUNG WOMEN OF LONDON

Is your "Best Boy" wearing Khaki? If not, don't you think he should be?

If he does not think that you and your country are worth fighting for—do you think he is worthy of you?

Don't pity the girl who is alone—her young man is probably a soldier—fighting for her and her country—and for you.

If your young man neglects his duty to his King and Country, the
time may come when he will neglect you. Think it over—then ask
your young man to

JOIN THE ARMY TO-DAY[7]

By the first Christmas of the war the soldiers were already expressing their
frustration. The Germans in particular deplored the idea of fighting during
a festival they regarded as a Germanic institution. When soldiers in the Royal
Saxon Regiment stationed between Frelinghien and Houplines put up little
Christmas trees decorated with lights, the Germans thought it was a surprise
attack and fired briefly on their lines, but the following morning the German
and English soldiers were exchanging cigarettes and chocolates, and later
they played football together. When the chiefs of staff heard about it they
issued orders that nothing similar was to be allowed to happen again.

In the new year the German line was still impenetrable. The aim of
the Allies was simply to "maneuver for position," since they knew that Germany had the advantage; its army already occupied most of Belgium and
large parts of Northern France. With the French troops still attempting to
block the invasion of Paris, it was they who bore the brunt of the battle in
the West. At the same time the British Expeditionary Force was hampered
in its attempts to gain ground in other parts of the front line; it was depen-
dent on the support, and therefore the redeployment, of French troops to
back up its offensive. The dominance of German troops in the North and
West, combined with their successful depletion of the Russian armies in
the East, encouraged Lord Hankey, Secretary to the War Council, to recognize the need for an alternative strategy: "The remarkable deadlock
which has occurred in the western theatre of war invites consideration
of the question whether some other outlet can be found for effective employment of the great forces of which we shall be able to dispose in a few months
time."[8]

The result of this thinking was a plan to reduce the power of enemy
forces by attacking them through their ally, the Turks. The idea was Winston
Churchill's brainchild: he argued that by removing Turkey from the war the
Allies would reduce the German strength from the South. Ian Hamilton,
Commander of the Mediterranean Expeditionary Force, agreed to an assault
on the Gallipoli peninsula. It was not possible to carry out the original plan,
and when Hamilton attacked on 22 March 1915 he was ill-prepared for a
battle by land and sea at the same time. The result was that further troops—
British, French, Australian, and New Zealander—were drafted in, but they
were not briefed about the objectives of the landing or the inevitable danger.
Few of the soldiers had experience in amphibious warfare, and they had no

suitable landing craft. They were an easy target for the Turks. The Allied forces established no more than a tentative foothold on the peninsula. In less than a fortnight the War Council was considering evacuation. Half the Allied forces became casualties. Nothing had been gained. In the course of the heated discussion as to who was responsible for this humiliating defeat, Winston Churchill resigned his post as First Lord of the Admiralty, but Ian Hamilton refused to accept any blame.

The British forces on the western front were demoralized by the knowledge that the Germans had suffered no defeat either in the East or in the South. The aim of the campaign in the trenches continued to consist of nothing more than to surprise the enemy and to break through the line. The Battle of Champagne dragged on through the winter months from January to March 1915. During all that time the French troops continued to attack; they succeeded in making small gains but no major breakthrough. It was becoming clear that the reason such heavy losses were sustained to no military advantage was that both sides were inexperienced in trench warfare, now rapidly becoming the dominant mode of combat. This inexperience was exacerbated by a popular misconception on the part of the commanders regarding the "Gap," a theory proposing that if the attacking forces could only make a gap in the enemy line, then wider penetration could lead to their eventual defeat. As the trenches became deeper and more complex on both sides, the likelihood of success for the "Gap" strategy became more remote, but belief in it fueled the drive for recruitment, since forces would have to break through the enemy lines in sufficient numbers to ensure the defeat of the enemy.

The combined French and British attacks in Picardy, Artois, and Champagne in early 1915 devastated the armies on both sides. Tear gas was used for the first time early in that year, but it was not until after 22 April, when the Germans used chlorine at Ypres, that the horror of this modern weapon became widely known. There were sustained failures at the second Ypres battle and at Gallipoli, Neuve Chapelle, Festubert, Arras, and Loos. The British troops in particular were unused to fighting on a narrow front. For many months the devastating loss of life was accepted as a necessary part of modern methods of war; the German poet Ivan Goll wrote in despair that "Whole regiments gambled away eternity for ten yards of wasteland,"[9] and E. A. Mackintosh, in the concluding line of his poem "Recruiting," bleakly declared, "Lads, you're wanted. Come and die."[10] Siegfried Sassoon described the experience in greater detail:

> Lines of grey, muttering faces, marked with fear,
> They leave their trenches, going over the top,
> While time ticks blank and busy on their wrists,
> And hope, with furtive eyes and grappling fists.
> Flanders in mud. O Jesus make it stop.[11]

While women poets could not ignore the subject of trench warfare, they wrote about it with less desperation and less detail and with more faith in eternal comfort. The following two poems by women are not atypical:

A SOLDIER'S FACE IN A STARTING TRAIN
With the turbulence and din
Of battle hammering near you, clipping you in;
A man's life as lightly going
As a wind's blowing;
Your life as like to be cut off as not
In the sore stress;
For all, be it much or little, that you gave,
God give you comfort in your inmost thought,
Vision and knowledge of what you fight to save,
And in that vision break your loneliness.[12]

THE SCARLET HARVEST
Fighting in the front rank, dying where they fell,
In the din and roar of battle, in the carnage that was Hell;
Writhing in their anguish with gaping wounds and gory,
Resting now in peace and everlasting glory.[13]

As women who supported the war effort and recruitment became aware of the scale of suffering and death resulting from trench warfare, their only recourse was to dignify the sacrifice by conferring an eternal weight of glory on those who died. But these and many other descriptions of war raised questions in the minds of both men and women as to the value of fighting a war in this way.

While the politically unaware supported the war with unquestioning patriotism, some had never accepted that it had any value. In its early months, the war was opposed by half the leading women in the British suffrage movement. On the day after war broke out, supporters of the suffrage movement held a peace meeting in London. The campaign for women's right to vote thus developed into the peace movement. Perhaps the most striking example of this convergence was the International Women's Congress held at The Hague on 27 April 1915, which was at times attended by as many as 2,000 delegates. While armies were involved in bloody, attritional warfare, women were offering a powerful demonstration of their ability to organize themselves and to issue a definitive statement demanding peace. Resolutions were also passed that autonomy and a democratic parliament should not be refused to any people, that women should be granted equal political rights with men, and that there should be democratic control of foreign policy, with no secret treaties; there was also a request for universal disarmament. These resolutions were consciously taken in a context of war and its consequent suffering: "We had one [delegate] who learned that her son had been killed and women who had learned two days earlier that their husbands had been killed, and women who had come from belligerent countries full of the unspeakable horror, of the physical horror of war, these women sat there with their anguish and sorrows, quiet, superb, poised, and with only one thought, 'What can we do to save the others from similar sorrow?' "[14]

The mood was optimistic and determined, and the outcome was a personal triumph for the Hungarian feminist Rosika Schwimmer. She proposed that the 20 resolutions agreed upon should not remain "paper expression of pious wishes" but should be springboards for international action; to this end she urged the Congress to elect some of its delegates as envoys to carry the resolutions in person to the heads of "belligerent and neutral governments and to the President of the United States." When the British feminist Chrystal Macmillan attempted to amend the proposal by suggesting that American social worker Jane Addams and Dutch suffragist Aletta Jacobs visit the appropriate ambassadors at The Hague, Addams responded by saying that the Schwimmer resolution was "melodramatic and absurd."[15] But Schwimmer persevered and asked to be allowed to speak again. Her speech included these words: "Brains—they say—have ruled the world till to-day. If brains have brought us to what we are in now, I think it is time to allow our hearts to speak. When our sons are killed by millions, let us, mothers, only try to do good by going to kings and emperors, without any other danger than a refusal!"[16] It was necessary to count the vote twice, but it was carried with loud applause.

After the Hague Conference, the women's and pacifist movements became even more closely allied. Before the war there were 600 Women's Suffrage Societies in Great Britain, led by Millicent Garrett Fawcett, and 100,000 affiliated suffragists; after the outbreak of the war, 800 new members were enrolling a month. One of the leading English suffragists was Charlotte Despard, dubbed "the grandmother of the revolution."[17] Ironically, her brother was Field Marshal Sir John French, commander of the British Expeditionary Forces in France. His failure to achieve any success in the first year of war would result in his removal from the front and his replacement by Sir Douglas Haig.

Haig was responsible for four major assaults on the German line in 1915; at Neuve Chapelle (10–12 March), Auberts Ridge (9 May), Festubert (15–27 May), and Loos (25 September–8 October). He planned each of these assaults meticulously and took care to ensure that the troops to be involved in the attack were withdrawn prior to the assault for further training. In spite of these carefully organized maneuvers, the British Expeditionary Force suffered a series of defeats; the plain truth was that by autumn 1915 the British offensive had failed. While the women at the Hague Conference were discussing peace, those fighting at the front were coming to the realization that the Germans had greater resources and better training, which enabled them to regroup and counterattack, while the British had neither the quantity nor the quality of guns to defeat them.

Nonetheless, the British offensives of 1915 were, on analysis, experimental, and it would be wrong to say that their failure was total. On the first day of the Battle of Neuve Chapelle and on the first day at Loos, General Haig's troops succeeded in penetrating the enemy line and thus shifting the battle-ground. At Neuve Chapelle it was not possible to follow up the breakthrough, because the High Command did not hear of the success until it was too late to commit further resources and thus secure the gains made. In the Battle of Loos, Haig asked Sir John French to arrange for reserves to be held close to the rear of the First Army's attacking forces, but these troops were not put in place and so the impressive gains made by the Fifteenth (Scottish) Division—they advanced on the German lines to a depth of 3,000 yards by 9 A.M. on the first morning of the battle—were never turned into a major victory. The forward movement was achieved with heavy losses, and at the moment of attack the troops were too tired and disoriented to exploit their success. Sir John French attempted to cover up the disaster by publishing a dispatch in the *Times* of 2 November 1915 that gave inaccurate information about the release of reserves. His feeble cover-up fueled the growing doubts about his ability to continue in a position of high command. Haig had already complained to Kitchener (British Secretary for War, 1914–16) about French's conduct at Loos, and on 8 December 1915 Haig was asked to succeed French as British Commander in Chief.

Haig's lack of imagination and inflexible approach to the developments of the war served only to further the problems of entrenchment. The events of 1915 had strengthened the position of the German army, and the battles of that year had produced neither peace nor victory for either side. The only way forward was considered to be a large-scale Allied offensive on all fronts. But the difficulty of arriving at a united strategy was already apparent. Lloyd George summed up the situation thus: "The trouble with Allied strategy was that there wasn't one."[18] There was no agreement among or within the countries in the Allied forces. The isolation and vulnerability of the French troops continued to be a problem for any coordinated Allied offensive. In early 1916 Gen. Joseph Joffre and the French military force were still engaged at Verdun and were therefore not in a position to give the kind of support required to the British Expeditionary Force. The British troops had been well trained in preparation for the Battle of the Somme, but badly needed reinforcements from the French to secure a decisive victory.

The Battle of the Somme began on 1 July 1916; the day was hot; 14 British divisions were ordered to leave their trenches and advance toward the German line. As always, there was to be no turning back. By evening there were 57,000 casualties, 20,000 of them fatal. This death toll was more than the entire strength of the German frontline garrison at the beginning of battle. The Battle of the Somme was to last for another 140 days. Kitchener's "New Army" accounted for 60 percent of those who were recruited; Kitchener had promised that those who "joined together" should "serve together." They did more—they died together. It has truly been said that while the British army recovered, the British nation never did.

In the Battle of the Somme, General Haig hoped to take over the German trench system and to achieve a breakthrough that would in turn allow his cavalry to pass through into open country and defeat the Germans in the North. There was some success in the South, virtual stalemate and sometimes defeat in the North, and no breakthrough at all in the center, where success had been most desired. Erich von Falkenhayn, the German Minister for War, had made up his mind that the enemy should be made to advance over dead bodies. Once the scale of the losses was known, Haig could have stopped this course of action and determined on a different strategy. But it was not in his nature to rethink military strategy or change the deployment of troops once they had been established. Haig introduced the tank as a "secret weapon" in September, and fighting continued through October. Very little was gained; the battle finally came to an end with a heavy frost and a snow-storm on 18 November. Three million men fought at the Somme and 1 million became casualties; half a million were German, 400,000 British, and 200,000 French. The most significant advance was eight miles. Lloyd George de-scribed it as one of the "most gigantic, tenacious, grim, futile and bloody fights ever waged in the history of war."[19]

During the Battle of the Somme two soldiers would stand back to back to sleep while a third stood guard to make sure they did not fall into the mud. Meanwhile, behind the lines, nurses too fell asleep on duty and so did ambulance drivers, men and women. It was a woman who wrote, "We were quite worn out, and the drivers were absolutely exhausted as well. My driver fell asleep one night when we had a terrible load of badly wounded men. It was the middle of the night and the ambulance went right up on the pavement with a great lurch and then banged down again."[20] Nurses describe having to hold the stumps of recently amputated legs in an attempt to alleviate the pain during the long ambulance drives undertaken to enable badly wounded men to return to England more quickly. Nurses stationed in the hospitals had to work to a strict and disciplined routine: "I don't like my ward. The only thing that really matters is that the beds are tidy, and at every odd minute the sister sends me off to tuck the blankets in more tightly, no matter if the man is sleeping or has a hideous wound which every movement jars. A convoy came in one night and we have a gunner with both legs off. He had to have his first dressing off with gas, and that made him struggle so they haven't been able to give it again and the pain he has is horrible."[21]

The above extract is from one of many accounts of the strain of nursing the thousands of soldiers wounded on the Somme. The nurses had to work around the clock and observe the strict orders given by the nursing sisters and their superiors. The soldiers were wounded and dying because they had obeyed orders, and the nurses who served them were also working under military discipline. "The men were so anxious to talk to us, just to be friendly, but it was strictly against the rules. It wasn't 'done' for them to come to Sister's bunk. That was sacrosanct. Some of these older Sisters, well, they weren't really human, we used to think. Of course, we were very young, but we perhaps had more regard for these men; we were sorry for them and there was no harm in it at all. It was completely innocent but it was against the rules so that was that."[22]

Even before the Somme the conditions inside the trenches were proving as treacherous as those facing the soldiers going over the top. Rats were everywhere, and lice multiplied in the seams of garments. Charles Delvert wrote in his diary entry for 12 January 1916 this description of conditions: "Lights out. Now the rats and the lice are the masters of the house. You can hear the rats nibbling, running, jumping, rushing from plank to plank, emitting their little squeals behind the dugout's corrugated metal. It's a noisy swarming activity that just won't stop. At any moment I expect one to land on my nose. And then it is the lice and fleas that begin to devour me. Absolutely impossible to get any shut-eye."[23] The smell of decomposition was pervasive, clouds of flies settled on the corpses, and mud and filth clung to everything in the dugout. Wilfred Owen captured the experience vividly:

> Tonight, this frost will fasten on this mud and us
> Shrivelling many hands, puckering foreheads crisp.
> The burying party, picks and shovels in the shaking grasp,
> Pause over half-known faces. All their eyes are ice,
> But nothing happens.[24]

The Battle of the Somme had reduced both sides until, in the mud, men were no longer recognizable.

On 1 January 1917 Haig was elevated to the rank of field marshal, and Bapaume, which had been one of the first objectives of the fighting on the Somme, was captured. In April the British troops continued with their offensive and pressed on with their attack for five days, gaining 7,000 yards at a cost of 160,000 killed and wounded. On 7 June a new tactic was used: British sappers tunneled underneath the German lines, and at 3:10 A.M. the mines they had laid were set off. This attack had been brilliantly planned by Gen. Sir Herbert Plummer, who had had the insight to discover a means to surprise the enemy. The German lines were thrown into confusion by the explosions, which killed 10,000 soldiers and caused another 7,000 to be captured. The British army advanced with 72 tanks on a 10-mile front and eventually occupied Vimy Ridge.

Haig had always favored the Flanders fields as a strategic battleground. The third Ypres battle, more popularly referred to as Passchendale, was not initiated by the British solely for the sake of drawing fire away from the weakened French forces but as a means of gaining ground and of forging a way ahead to take the ports of Ostend and Zeebrugge, which would thus make a naval victory more secure. After the depletion of the French army at the Somme, morale was low and a wave of mutinies exacerbated an already desperate situation. The French army did make a significant recovery, however, and it was engaged in a new offensive at Verdun as early as 20 August; but on 23 October a successful attack was made against the Chemin des Dames. As Haig saw it, the Flanders campaign of the summer and autumn of 1917 was the only way forward, but, again, no strategic objective was achieved.

The taking of Passchendale had been Haig's main objective, but the campaign was severely criticized: the choice of battlefield, the strategy, the tactics, and the choice of battlefield commander. It was followed by a further British offensive in November against the German line near Cambrai. There was a successful tank attack by the British, when 7,500 German prisoners and 120 guns were taken and the German front was pushed back by 7,000 yards. This was the most significant advance made along the front. The gain, however, was short-lived; the Allied forces were exhausted and the Germans gathered strength and counterattacked, winning back all the ground they had lost. This setback revealed a strategic failure in the coordination of tanks and ground troops, but from the viewpoint of the soldiers still engaged in the war, the crippling loss of life and the terror of continued fighting were far more damaging. Soon after the trench system had been created, the British, French, and German armies in turn had tried to break the deadlock, but in turn each failed. This impasse continued into the third year of the war, and the use of tanks in 1917 made the prospect of further combat still more frightening. It could truthfully be said that in the summer of 1917 400,000 men were killed for nothing.

The failure of the Flanders campaign took a further heavy toll on confidence, which was already seriously depleted, and during the summer of 1917 desertions continued to rise among both the German and Allied armies. Many thousands of German soldiers fled to Holland, whose neutrality gave them at least a temporary hiding place. It seemed to the generals of both sides that it was necessary to plan further battles along the western front, even though past experience had proved that it would not bring a decisive conclusion to the fighting. The way ahead pointed to the development of a more complex strategy. More sophisticated methods were used: target acquisition, sound ranging, flash spotting, and aerial photography. Care was taken to camouflage guns and weaponry. Gen. Erich Ludendorff, who had succeeded Falkenhayn as German Minister for War, fixed the first day of spring, 21 March 1918, as the day of attack. At 4:40 A.M. the German spring offensive began with a heavy bombardment of the Allied lines. The advance was decisive: the German army took Ham, Bapaume, Peronne, Nesle, Noyou, and Albert in a week, and by 27 March the British were forced to retreat to a position farther back than that from which they had started in 1916. The major networks of communication appeared to be about to fall into the hands of the German army, now within 12 miles of the city of Amiens and its powerful railway system. Suddenly, German victory seemed within sight. Haig made the protection of Amiens his main objective, and on 25 March called for the French Marshal, Ferdinand Foch, to direct the action of all the Allied armies on the western front.

Under Ludendorff's direction, the German army continued its offensive with a two-pronged attack on the Ypres salient and pressed its advantage. On 6 April the German Sixth Army broke through the Allied line for a distance of three and a half miles up to the Lys River. The British Second Army was forced to retreat, and the Germans crossed the Lys. As events turned out, this was to be the last ground the Germans were able to gain without fatal consequences. On 11 April Haig issued his "backs to the wall" Order of the Day, a desperate instruction to hold the line at all costs and to attempt no offensive action. The Passchendale Ridge, so dearly bought, was abandoned by the British, and the French lost Kemmel Hill. The line had to be reduced again on 26–27 April, marking the last-ditch stand of the British Expeditionary Force. The question of the control of the English Channel ports was still moot, but as the German army advanced toward the end of April they were repelled by heavy artillery fire. Though the Germans still showed more technical skill than the Allies in trench warfare, they had failed to secure their positions on the Somme or in Flanders. The campaigns of 1917 and early 1918 had resulted in the depletion of Allied troops and the continued lowering of morale. In addition, some men were required to return to civilian jobs to boost the economy at home. Haig estimated that he would be as many as 248,226 men short by 31 March 1918. The army was redistributed into 9 divisions instead of 12 battalions; the result was that the new force had greater responsibilities and was asked to take over a section of the French line. It was also agreed that the line would be extended by 28 miles. Although the regroupings seemed awkward and disorienting at the time, they eventually proved to be part of a winning strategy. The other ingredient that contributed to victory for the Allied forces was the defeat of Turkey, an objective that had been more clearly in focus at the start of the war.

During May and June the Germans advanced near the Lys and Marne Rivers, but as the experience of war had already shown, the successful attack invariably debilitated the troops, and the German army was sapped of strength by the late summer of 1918. It could be said that it was all but defeated by the end of July, but it was still necessary for the Allies to prove their victory, with the final defeat occurring at the front where the war had started. Between 8 August and 11 November a series of battles, planned and executed by Haig, brought about the Allied victory. The decisive turning point came with the arrival of American troops, flooding in to France at the rate of

150,000 a month. The fresh energy they supplied in September at St.-Mihiel salient caused the final collapse of the German army. In early October the German government offered an armistice to President Woodrow Wilson, and as a result the Allies were able to begin negotiations calling for an end to unrestricted submarine warfare and the German withdrawal from occupied territory. When the Armistice was signed on 11 November 1918, the war had cost Germany and the Central Powers 3.5 million lives and the Allies more than 5 million.

== The Paradoxes of War ==

In 1914 the women of England joined forces to send their men to war, and in the winter of 1915 white feathers were handed out to those men who had still not joined up. Yet by 1918 the same women were seeking some kind of revenge for the staggering loss of life that was the legacy of war. In particular, the Battle of the Somme was felt to have broken the back of English manhood, shattered Western culture, and caused women to reconsider their position and future in a world that had suddenly changed.

Women's involvement in the war brought to the surface a number of paradoxes. In 1914 certain German feminists made it clear that they considered men to blame for the declaration of war, arguing that a feminist understanding of the value of human life would not have permitted such a step. It was, they believed, up to women to reveal the nature of men's belligerence and, if necessary, to take up arms against them to bring an end to their imperialism and their wars.[25] Yet, simultaneously, the war was to provide women with an opportunity to demonstrate their ability to work alongside men on equal terms.

In July 1914 there were 3.25 million British women workers; at the end of the war there were 5 million. In France, by late 1918 half a million women alone were directly employed in defense industries. At the height of the war, Colonel Joffre remarked, "If the women in war factories stopped for 20 minutes we should lose the War."[26] Nor was the situation any different in Germany. The war thus involved the women of opposing nations in supporting a conflict they also wanted to stop.

The majority of women before 1914 had accepted traditional social values and did not want political change. But for them, too, the war challenged their notion of their roles and responsibilities. Woman suffrage, which had been feared, now took on a different significance. World War I saw the death of the emancipation movement, which had concerned itself with the wider issues of equity, along with the demise of the Liberal government, and the subsequent rise of the suffrage movement, which had the more political objective of gaining the vote. Between 1890 and 1910 the emancipation movement had challenged the long-established notion that women lived only in relation to men: that marriage was the accepted path and that a woman's security was bound up in her husband. Georgian feminists struck out for an unprecedented independence. They looked on men as inferior and reacted against the traditional roles available to women. A number of different social and political organizations headed by women worked to further the cause of emancipation. They were led by the Women's Social and Political Union and the National Union of Women's Suffrage, which joined forces to provide a more concerted campaign for peace and woman suffrage.

Inevitably the demand for the vote increased and with it the hope that the female voice might be heard as a political and public force for peace and equality. This was the spirit of the international conference at The Hague, where the demands for world peace were thoroughly debated by leading suffragists and pacifists.

It could be argued that the woman suffrage in Great Britain would have been accomplished sooner had war not been declared in 1914. The weakened position of the Liberal government, which was in power only through the support of the new and growing Labour party, led it to consider extending the franchise to women in order to bolster its political base. The war changed the political climate; a coalition government did not need to woo women; issues of woman suffrage became less important than victory over the Germans. When women's right to vote was finally granted in 1918, it was in part a recognition of the work they had done during the war.

Women had driven ambulances and trams, heaved coal, and made munitions; one group of women had built a shipyard. The growth and range of employment opportunities for women accelerated as the war progressed. In June 1915 the *Daily Mail* listed the many occupations taken up by women: they were tram conductors, lift attendants, shopwalkers, bookstall clerks, ticket collectors, motor-van drivers, van guards, milk deliverers, railway carriage cleaners, window cleaners, dairy workers, and shell makers.[27] Women had become arc welders, aeronautical engineers, and airship builders. Initially dependant on the skills of men to enable them to carry out these jobs, they had by the end of the war learned to make their own tools and to set their own machines. In 1916 Mrs. Churchill wrote in her book *Women's War Work*, "It is one of the virtues of war that it puts the light which in peacetime is hid under a bushel in such prominence that all can see it."[28] The *Daily Mail* made the point that women's work in wartime was providing them with a greater freedom and independence: "The wartime business girl is to be seen any night dining out alone or with a friend in the moderate-priced restaurants in London. Formerly she would never have had her evening meal in town unless in the company of a man friend. But now with money and without men she is more and more beginning to dine out."

Women's response to the nature of their new employment was, understandably, ambivalent. While a number of them spoke with pride about their war work, many confessed that they would not wish to do it again. One woman working in a projectile factory wrote in a prize-winning essay, "the fact that I am using my life's energy to destroy human souls gets on my nerves. Yet on the other hand, I'm doing what I can to bring this horrible affair to an end. But once the War is over, never in creation will I do the same thing again."[29] Although women employed as nurses, drivers, or factory workers did not find themselves in this quandary, women who worked during this period—in whatever capacity—viewed their "war work" as different from "normal" employment.

The growth of women's political consciousness went hand in hand with their experience of war work. Lloyd George was made Minister of Munitions in 1915, and his policies were in part responsible for this development. As early as December 1914 he outlined his proposals for "dilution," which opened up employment for women by placing semiskilled or unskilled women in jobs formerly reserved for skilled men. Under Lloyd George, the Ministry of Munitions took over certain factories involved in war production and also built new, state-owned factories. The number of women employed in munitions production rose from 82,589 in July 1914 to 340,844 by July 1916 and to 1,587,300 by November 1918.[30] Lloyd George saw women as essential to the work force, saying, "Without women victory will tarry, and the victory which tarries means a victory whose footprints are footprints of blood."[31] Although he declared his commitment to women's employment, he was ambivalent about terms and conditions, explaining that women would not do quite the same work as men and should therefore be paid less. Predictably, this brought women into conflict with the trade unions over the issue of a fair rate of pay. The overall effect of "dilution" was to challenge both male and female roles in the labor market and to enlarge women's experience of industrial organization and involvement with trade unions.

Next to work in munitions, the recruitment of women to the army was one of the most contentious forms of war work. After Lt. Gen. H. M. Lawson's report of 16 January 1917, which outlined the need for, and the means of achieving, employment for women in the army in France, the idea was accepted in principle. In practice, however, it was hedged about with difficulties. Sir Douglas Haig said there was "a limit with regard to the extent to which replacement [of those who had died] by unfit men, women and coloured labour can be carried out with safety."[32] But even as Haig was voicing this reactionary sentiment, the wheels were in motion for the recruitment of women into the army. Selection boards were being set up and recruitment carried on through the office of the Director General of National Service. The entrance requirements were two references and an appearance before a medical board on which all the doctors were women. The volume of applications exceeded the number of available places. The distrust of women's capabilities implicit in Haig's pronouncement was made explicit when, early on in the establishment of the Women's Army Auxiliary Corps (WAAC) of the British Army, it was decided that commissions would be given only to men;

instead of officers, women would be controllers and administrators, and instead of NCOs, they would be forewomen. It was not long, though, before the WAAC developed its own distinctive hierarchy and system of ranking with appropriate rewards.

The objection to women's involvement in military service was that women should not be used at the front to fight and kill. This was a male preserve. Women in military uniform were described as "aping" men, which was not to be encouraged.

> Near these ridiculous "poseuses" stood the real thing—a British officer in mufti. He had lost his left arm and right leg . . . surely if these women had a spark of shame left they should have blushed to be seen wearing a parody of the uniform which this officer and thousands like him have made a symbol of honour and glory by their deeds. I do not know the corps to which these ladies belong, but if they cannot become nurses or ward maids in hospital, let them put on sunbonnets and print frocks and go and make hay or pick fruit or make jam, or do the thousand and one things that women can do to help. But, for heaven's sake, don't let them ride and march about the country making themselves and, what is more important, the King's Uniform ridiculous.[33]

This passage from the *Morning Post* relies on an almost atavistic hint that women might suffer equal physical mutilation and reinforces the belief that their more important function was to send men to the front to fight and be killed.

The consensus was often expressed in these terms: if women were needed to do men's work during the war, that might have to be accepted as a temporary expedient; but women should not take on the "real" work or role of men. While this attitude was frequently accepted by women employed on the home front, it was different for the women working close to the front line. Whether bandaging the wounded, driving ambulances, or working in the Women's Army Auxiliary Corps, the women employed there did not feel themselves to be mere substitutes for men.

Dame Katherine Furse, Commandant of the Women's Voluntary Aid Detachments (VADs), a voluntary organization of nursing staff prepared to work behind the lines, wanted close cooperation between the WAAC and the VADs. Her overtures for cooperation were met with resistance, and the alternative suggestion was put forward by many influential members of the government that the VADs should be absorbed into the WAAC. This would not only have had the effect of diluting both organizations and greatly diminishing their individual strengths, it would have meant that VAD work would come under the ultimate control of men. Dame Katherine refused to accept any such move, making the seemingly unfortunate claim that "V.A.D. work is entirely for the sick and wounded. All such work is eminently the work of women."[34] Her point was more significant than appears; she was determined to maintain the exclusive female control of the VADs and to defend its distinctive contribution to the war. She perceived the political dimension of what was in essence a battle between male and female control of organizations. The VADs held their position, and after the WAAC was established the Womens' Royal Naval Service (WRNS) was created in 1917 and the Women's Royal Auxiliary Airforce in 1918. World War I established the identity and purpose of women in the armed forces; there they used the skills as engineers, mechanics, and electricians they had developed at an earlier stage of the war effort through their employment in these spheres as civilians. In recognition of Dame Katherine's determination to hold her ground concerning the distinctive nature of women's work in the war, she was made Commandant in Chief of the WRNS.

By 1920 two thirds of the women who had been employed during the war had left their jobs. The state put its seal of approval on the exodus of women from the workplace to return to the home, with married women in particular encouraged to leave. The idea of "mothers' pensions" was put forward by the Trades Unions Congress as a means of encouraging women to rear children rather than to work. The traditional female role was expressed in terms of vocation—an essential calling to build up family life: "A call comes again to the women of Britain, a call happily not to make shells or fill them so that a ruthless enemy can be destroyed but a call to help renew the homes of England, to sew and to mend, to cook and to clean and to rear babies in health and happiness, who shall in their turn grow into men and women worthy of the Empire."[35] Although there was a large-scale return to home and hearth, women had become more discerning about the terms and conditions of work. Their brushes with trade unions during the war had done much to sharpen their political astuteness; their training and work experience had enhanced their future employment prospects. The simple figures for women's postwar paid employment do not reveal the true story; their work experiences during the war had a profound impact on future expectations and patterns of employment.

Women's Voices

Many different accounts of World War I have been outlined in history books, but few give space to the views and experiences of the women who worked alongside men to win the war. Women's war experience was novel, challenging, and more varied than that of men. Without models, they often did not know the appropriate response to their new circumstances. For many nurses treating the wounded, the whole of the war was arcane, something they should not and did not want to know about. Some viewed the war as a temporary interlude in normal life and chose to ignore its more serious effects.

Other women were deeply shaken by the suffering of the soldiers and entered into their pain. Before the Battle of the Somme, most of the documentary material available from those women working behind the lines was matter-of-fact and accepting; after the Somme, there was a much greater questioning and sense of hopelessness—a change of attitude that can also be seen in the poetry written by men during the war. Women's initial patriotic enthusiasm was tempered by the reality of the casualty lists, and the resulting depression and hopelessness were eventually succeeded by a determination to win the war.

The work women did at the front and their accounts of it defy categorization; it is better that they should speak for themselves. An enormous amount of writing took place—letters, journals, diaries, memoirs; and some of it became the raw material for fiction during and after the war. Ways in which the private voice modulated into public and published voices are also discussed in greater detail in chapter 5. Here, to set the scene and redress the balance of a war accounted for by men through the battles they fought, are the authentic voices of the women who worked with them. The fact that they were not intended for publication gives them an unconsidered directness and immediacy.

The range of women's responses to their war work is wide. The nurses, who were dealing with immediate needs, were not always very reflective. Many nurses came to their work with little or no idea as to the details of battle, and few were curious. They prepared the hospitals and tended the wounded. Dorothy Littlejohn, who was a cook with the Scottish Women's Hospitals in France in 1914–15, wrote to her fiancé about her work: "Get up at 6.30am wash in water out of hot water bottle and a little water for our teeth in my thermos. In the kitchen at 7am to see that the porridge is on, kettles and coffee. Send up the Doctor's breakfast at 8am: Coffee bread and butter. Prayers at 8.20am at 8.30–9 clear the kitchen. Lunch at 12–12.30 doctors dinner at 7pm and our supper at 7.45pm after supper there is the clearing up . . . I am really busy in an uninteresting way."[36] Her letters go on to say how the world of the hospital is so different from either England or the front that it is hard to understand what is going on. But at this stage of the war certain views are fairly firmly held: "They are having a good deal of trouble with their motors; they don't know whether women are to be allowed to drive them or not," she writes. "Myself I think it is a perfectly mad idea to think of letting women drive."

Behind the lines, VADs adopted a purely supportive role and they, too, often asked no questions. They did sacrificial and gruesome work in the knowledge that it was expedient and temporary. Many, of whom Dorothy Littlejohn is one example, described their world as enclosed and self-contained, cut off from the action. Often letters home describe trivial things—flowers, friends, and food—to avoid mentioning the war. The letters of Miss D. E. Higgins, stationed at the Anglo-Belgian Hospital in Rouen, to her parents in Lincolnshire provide hardly any detail of the horrific nature of her work as a nurse; there is only a stray light-hearted comment: "This awful War does take the starch out of life and one wonders how it is to go on." She avoids the subject of war and writes more about social life in England, asking about the parties that are still taking place and about the welfare of friends of the family. She writes about the leave she is planning and says she is determined to come home to do some gardening: "Now don't begin to worry about the U-boats; everyone is taking leave as usual, and if I don't snatch my chance now heaven alone knows when I shall get any leave. I shall prune all the roses and spend your birthday with you which shall be ripping."[37] Her letters so obviously refuse to allow the weight of circumstance and the unpleasantness of war to intrude upon her sense of connection with her life in England. Reading her letters, it is quite difficult to remember that she served as VAD from February 1916 to June 1917.

A good many of the horrors that came direct from the fighting were absorbed behind the lines, where the nursing staff was too affected, too busy, or too tired to record them. The accounts of the injuries and the condition of the men were invariably more graphic when described by the nurses who received the wounded from the ambulance trains.

> The worst case I saw—and it still haunts me—was of a man being carried past us. It was night, and in the dim light I thought that his face was covered with a black cloth. But as he came nearer, I was horrified to realise that the whole lower half of his face had been completely blown off and what appeared to be a huge gaping black hole. That was the only time that I nearly fainted on the platform, but fortunately I was able to pull myself together. It was the most frightful sight because it could not be covered up at all.[38]

Many soldiers who were seriously wounded but fit enough to travel came to England for treatment. Sister Henrietta Hall at St. Luke's Military Hospital in Bradford wrote, "I remember one particular Cornish I was very sorry for. He had been gassed at Ypres and had been with us a long time. He was absolutely terrified of going back to the front—because he was almost well again—and he used to beg me to let him off going."[39] Accounts like this and descriptions of wounds, conditions, and states of health are endless. And as the stream of casualties increased, so there developed a growing sense of helplessness.

In the evidence available in the Archives of the Imperial War Museum it is also clear that there is a distinct difference in style between letters written from France and diaries written in England at the same time recording similar events. The physical condition of the wounded is not often the subject of letters home from France. More attention is given to describing the people who work in the hospitals than to those who lie dying, to the difficulties of treating the wounded than to their state of health. The nurses serving in England, however, often write freer and franker accounts. The following statement from Sister Grace Buffard, who worked at the General Hospital in Rouen, is characteristic of the tendency of those close to the suffering to concentrate on the problems of treatment rather than talk about the wounded:

> We had a tremendous number of men in that winter with chest trouble, and it wasn't so very easy to treat them in those conditions because all our basic training didn't apply. In a proper hospital when you make a linseed poultice, you close all the windows and see that there are no draughts before you make it so that it will stay really hot when you can put it on the patient, and will do the most good. I remember standing looking round the tent and thinking, "How on earth can you close all the windows—there aren't any?" We just had to do the best we could.[40]

This kind of practical, determinedly unemotional writing is echoed in the following account by Kathleen Yarwood when she describes how frostbite was treated. It is the treatment rather than the state of the feet, let alone the patient, that is described.

> Some of the trench feet and frostbite cases were so bad that they had to be sent home. We had a tremendous number of frostbite cases at the beginning of 1917. In fact we had a whole ward of them, and another nurse and myself were in charge of that for quite a long time. We had to rub their feet every morning and every evening with warm olive oil for about a quarter of an hour or so, massage it well in and wrap their feet in cotton wool and oiled silk—all sorts of things just to keep them warm—and then we put big fisherman's socks on them.[41]

The accounts of the influenza epidemic of 1918 produced cries of even greater helplessness, since there was no treatment and usually no cure. Margaret Ellis, who was a special military probationer at No. 26 General Hospital in Etaples, wrote: "It was a terrible epidemic. There was so little that we could do for them. The only treatment opportunity was to keep an even temperature in the ward, that was the main thing we were told. We just had to give them fluids and keep walking up and down seeing if anybody wanted anything. They were all incontinent so you were continually changing beds and washing."[42] The tragedy of the flu epidemic was that it struck so many who otherwise might have survived the war. It caused more deaths than the war and seemed to be the final offensive against the healthy. In the very last stages of the war, Margaret Ellis wrote, "You couldn't keep pace with the deaths. You'd just walk down the ward and see that another one had died. I've hated the sight of the Union Jack ever since, because they always used one to cover them as they carried them out on a stretcher."[43] Many nurses described death as a relief; for serious cases throughout the war and during the flu epidemic, they frequently had no appropriate treatment. Often they could only stand by and watch the patients suffer and die. Death in combat in some ways appeared the more merciful.

Witnessing the brutal and senseless slaughter or willful maiming of civilians in Belgium elicited a different response. Here the factual recording of details has the clearly perceived function of creating an evidential record: "The first village we came to was St Trond where the day before, the 'cultured' Germans by way of frightening the inhabitants into submitting to their orders and will had cut off or else cut right through the tendons of the children's hands from infants up to the age of sixteen." These and other horrific details of the war were recorded by Miss G. Holland, who compiled a 300-page journal illustrated with press cuttings, photographs, and original documents covering her experiences as an ambulance driver in Belgium in September–October 1914 and in France in November–December 1914; in the summer of 1915 she began to work in Serbia. Her journal records both minor and major incidents. At Malines she described a fairly minor one to illustrate the brutality of the German occupation: "I met an old lady here who worked constantly doing what she could at the hospital and she told me that when the Germans first entered Malines she was walking down a hill with a basket of bread and meat upon her arm. Some German soldiers snatched the basket from her, knocked her down and then kicked and rolled her down the hill. She was not very seriously injured but frightfully badly bruised and shaken." Holland described how towns and villages were devastated during this time. German soldiers massacred and pillaged, and in one town the bodies were piled 15 feet high as a warning to nearby inhabitants. In her writing she never flinches from providing a precise and detailed account of events as she experienced them: "Every train that came in had hundreds of refugees on board and so great were the numbers, that tents had to be put up to shelter them. . . . In this tent huddled together were children with scarlet fever and measles, adults with typhoid and other catching illnesses, expectant mothers, not to mention influenza and bronchitis all mixed up with the rest."[44] There was no means of treating them as there was neither medicine nor staff. The most serious difficulty was the lack of tetanus serum and the terrible suffering that resulted. The lack of tetanus serum is mentioned in a number of letters written by VADs in Belgium.

Sybil Harry worked with French servicemen at the Hospice Mixte in Saumur. She wrote: "22.10.14. The orderlies are soldiers too mad or too bad to fight. . . . If I told you some things that come in here you would be horrified and it is just as well that England has not seen yet these remains of what were bright young men brought in to die in a few dreadful hours . . . there is quite enough tetanus and that is fearful—I never knew they suffered so terribly."[45] Sybil Harry did not shrink from describing the wounds treated and the problem of inadequate supplies.

Other women involved in the war were inquisitive about military affairs and the progress of the war. They often sought to work with men and to gain training alongside them. Irene Rathbone was one of these. A self-confessed feminist in her diaries, she found it difficult to find out what was happening on the front apart from the official reports supplied by the press. Her own private source of information was the soldiers she entertained at the YMCA rest camp at St. Valery sur Somme in June–October 1918. It would seem that it was only at this stage that the full details of the experience of the trenches were given to her. Toward the end of the war her diary provides a more informed picture: "August 26th Mon 1918. Two of the boys came to supper, Stacey and Richards who help us devotedly at the club and were very nice. Richards is Irish and talks the whole time at the rate of 80 miles an hour. He described his first bombing raid, the mess-up at Cambrai and the episodes of trench life in an extraordinarily vivid way."[46] In October, a month before the end of the war, Rathbone made the following entry:

> Captain Fairclough is evidently a splendid soldier and did awfully well on the Sept 2nd show. He got excited talking (his nerves have gone a bit—that's why they let him stay on) and gave me the most vivid picture I have ever had presented of the horror of going over the top and killing Germans—the excitement, the fear, the madness. For two days he said it seemed as though he were drunk, he remembers nothing of what he did. I listened fascinated, though I could hardly bear it. He then went on to cursing the staff generally and Gough in particular. He thinks the latter ought to have been shot like a private soldier in that he has on his hands the blood of 100,000 men. He told us stories of that criminal ass that made one's soul seethe.

The frankness of this entry was not something that would be found in the accounts of the early stages of the war.

One aspect of the war that was rarely recorded in diaries and journals is the opportunity for sexual freedom it offered to both men and women. Rathbone hints at this in her diaries. In one entry she describes how she and her friend Pussy went out with Fairclough and another officer called Payne:

> Pussy with Fairclough, & I with Payne. The poor thing gripped my arm like a vice all the way down, but beyond that behaved himself very well—I felt he was using every inch of self-control (How disappointing!! said Puss when I told her afterwards) which pleased me, although considering that he was going back to the Front the following morning, I would have allowed . . . well! Anyhow things didn't get beyond promises to write, & speculations as to when & where we should meet again. He is a dear brave thing—and full of the joie de vivre—I like him. They both came in to supper.

On a number of occasions Rathbone comes close to suggesting that a sexual indiscretion has taken place. During the war there was a loosening of sexual constraints, both heterosexual and homosexual. Sex became for many an escape from the horror of war, a way of affirming life in the face of death. The breakup of marriages and the readjustment to different relationships became an almost natural process as husbands were killed or lovers forgotten. The excitement of romance and the possibility of finding new meaning in life were welcomed in new alliances that would, it was hoped, eclipse the past and point a way to the future.

In the autobiographical novel *Bid Me to Live,* written by the poet Hilda Dolittle under her pen name, H. D., the author describes how she fell wildly in love with D. H. Lawrence, who was married, while her husband, Richard Aldington, was at the front. On Aldington's return he had an affair with Dorothy Yorke, with H. D.'s knowledge and partial consent. Lawrence did not reciprocate H. D.'s interest, and so she went off to live with Cecil Grey in Cornwall. The central theme of her book is a plea for a new form of expression, for life and for romance in the midst of death. D. H. Lawrence offered H. D. the potential for romance, even if it was unrealized, in that he "bade her to live" in a new way. This assertion of life was the justification for the breakup of more than a few established relationships.

For many women, of course, the war offered no possibility of romance. Their husbands, brothers, or fiancés were at the front, and they were working hard to maintain the war effort at home.

Of the kinds of work available on the home front, work in munitions factories, though hard, was considered preferable to domestic service. It brought in additional money, was free of the class connotations of domestic service, and more clearly contributed to the war effort. One worker wrote:

> I was in domestic service and "hated every minute of it" when war broke out, earning £2 month working from 6am to 9pm. So when the need came for women "war workers" my chance came to "out."
> I started on hand cutting shell fuses at the converted water works at the AC, Thames Ditton, Surrey. It entailed the finishing off by "hand dies" the machine cut thread on the fuses that held the powder for the big shells, so had to be very accurate so that the cap fitted perfectly. We worked twelve hours a day apart from the journey morning and night at Kingston-upon-Thames.[47]

Work in munitions factories could be as dangerous as fighting at the front. Shells often exploded in or near the factory, maiming and killing the workers and those nearby. David Mitchell, in his book *Women on the Warpath,* records this story:

> After six days in the factory at Hayes, near London, Mabel Lethbridge volunteered for service in the Danger Zone where the high explosives

were poured and packed into the shells. Only seventeen, she had lied to her mother about the kind of work she was doing, had lied about her age to get into the factory at all. . . . Toward the end of her shift, as Mabel gave the signal to lower and the "beater" descended on yet another shell, there was a frightful explosion. The workers were blown to bits or burned alive, and she was the sole survivor. Appallingly wounded, she was unconscious for ten days; her left leg was amputated, and surgeons cut and stitched and grated away at her shattered body.[48]

Many women worked in munitions factories in dangerous and damaging surroundings. Two women medical officers in the munitions factories reported on the effects of TNT on women workers, and their findings were published in *Lancet* on 12 August 1916. They described the following symptoms as being directly caused by work in munitions: "Throat and/or chest tight, sore, swollen and burning; coughing, sometimes a thick yellow phlegm with bitter taste; pain round the waist and in abdomen; nausea, vomiting, constipation at first, then diarrhoea; rashes and eruptions on skin. These could in turn lead to toxic symptoms: digestive, as in the irritative stage in jaundice; circulatory, giddiness, hot and cold flushes, swelling etc.; cerebral, drowsiness, loss of memory, disorders of sight; delirium, coma and convulsions."[49]

Women working in the factories and prone to these conditions were often referred to as canaries because of the yellow color of their skin, the result of TNT poisoning. Many women spent the whole of the war working in munitions. Others decided to have a change of occupation. The woman quoted above who left domestic service for the factory describes how after a while she found a different kind of war work for herself: "I left the A.C.s in 1916 for a much cleaner and lighter job at the 'Wireless' Teddington where they made the wireless boxes for the signallers in the communications lines in France. They were some of the first such instruments of wireless to be used in warfare, and no doubt the same as my husband was using as he gained his MM [Military Medal] mending the communication lines under heavy shell fire as a volunteer."[50]

The School of Women Signallers was established in 1915; it trained women to be signal instructors at a time when there was a shortage of male instructors. In the first group of students a dozen members of the school passed the army signaling test and held first- or second-class certificates. The signalers were trained to teach semaphore flags, morse flags, lamp, buzzer telegraph sounder, and other systems of communication. Mrs. Brunskill Reid, the school's administrator, explained the training: "This branch of women's work in war-time is now very active. The school contains over a dozen members who have passed the Army signalling test, and these are engaged daily in teaching one or another branch of signalling (or in giving extra coaching) to soldiers about to fight, convalescent soldiers returned from the Front, Cadets of Public School Officers Training Corps, Scouts, Guides, etc."[51] Signal training was an area of women's work that grew and flourished during World War I and was taken up again during World War II. It was generally performed by educated, middle-class women rather than working-class women.

As is demonstrated by the School of Women Signallers, the war exposed women to a working experience unlike anything they had known before. They experienced new types of work, different training hierarchies, and different social relationships. Many unpublished accounts describe the interest and novelty as well as the challenge and horror of war work. The least frequently documented form of women's work is what they did in the Land Army. Agricultural labor did not change, whether carried out in wartime or in peacetime. In London's Imperial War Museum Archives there is very little material on land work. One document stands out, however. It is a scrap of paper in a barely literate hand describing the enjoyment of sleeping under canvas on straw and eating moldy green ham.

Irene Rathbone's three diaries later became the source for a semiautobiographical novel, *We That Were Young*. Her account offers some of the most interesting reflections on work, on the position of women, on relationships, and on the effects of the war on each of these topics. She concludes one section of her diaries with these words: "I think I have now put down everything that is of importance, or that I want to remember in those days before War burst upon us so swiftly, that there was no time to think of reasons before it had caught us all in its cruel grip to be crushed & moulded by pain into very different people from what we were in those careless far-away days which we call 'before the War.' "[52]

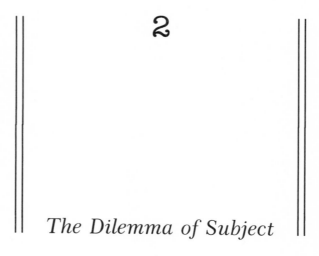

2

The Dilemma of Subject

From its start, the war was a stimulus to the imagination. Probably no other four years in history have produced as much testimony on public events.

—Modris Eksteins, *Rites of Spring*

It is not only that they celebrate male virtues, enforce male values and describe the world of men; it is that the emotion with which these books are permeated is to a woman incomprehensible.

—Virginia Woolf, *A Room of One's Own*

WHEN THE EXPERIENCES OF TWO GROUPS—WHETHER DIVIDED by color, age, class, or gender—are as disparate as those described in the previous chapter, two pitfalls to full understanding appear. The first is the temptation to contrast, rather than compare, the experiences. The second is to prioritize one experience as the central, the authentic, the real, and to make the other just that, "the other." Throughout this study we attempt to learn what we can from the similarity between men's and women's writing. Of at least equal importance, we do not use men's experience and men's writing as the norm against which women's experience and writing is judged.

= Authenticity =

To illustrate the danger of alterity, we can begin with a common critical attitude toward war writing, that it foregrounds authenticity, working within what Brian Murdoch calls an "inevitably historical framework."[1] Initially, nothing appears wrong with this statement. But how wide, how encompassing, is the framework? An uncritical acceptance of this attitude has meant that "literary scholars customarily exclude women's voices from the canon of war literature, favouring writings based on the actual experience of combat."[2] The even-handed attitude implicit in referring without prejudice to "non-participants" (Scott Fitzgerald, Katherine Anne Porter, and Dalton Trumbo, for example) writing "about the negative effects of war with angry conviction"[3] is rare. But even this attitude implicitly equates participation with combat. The war must be seen in all its ramifications, all its implications, if we are to be able to judge its impact—whether historical, social, or literary—properly.

Jean Bethke Elshtain expands on the reason for the predominance of such a narrow perspective while confirming the narrative authority bestowed by experience: "Because women are *exterior* to war, men *interior,* men have long been the great war story tellers, legitimated in that role because they have 'been there' or because they have greater entrée into what it 'must be like' . . . [they are] authorized to '*narrate.*' "[4] Yet even this perceptive analyst can confuse the experience of war in its wider sense with experience of combat and revert to the conventional position, as when she dismisses Edith Wharton's nonfiction account of traveling through the war-torn countryside, *Fighting France.* She claims that Wharton had no way to measure her imaginative reconstruction of the meaning of the war "against concrete experiences. She and the war passed one another by, as frequently happens for *noncombatants* who are not pressed upon as war *fighters* are" (emphasis added).[5] Wharton was not only a sophisticated travel writer, knowledgeable about the culture of the land in which she traveled, but France had become her home. This included the war years, when she was a committed war worker (for her many achievements in this sphere she was subsequently awarded the Legion d'Honneur), when she lost friends, endured aerial bombardments, and suffered with her adopted country. She was well able to draw on "concrete experiences" and adapt them to her new subject, but this is not considered to provide even partial credentials for her role as war writer. It will be a constant element in what follows that narratives of the war properly include writing from the home front and from occupied territory as well as postwar reassessments and reevaluations.

The attitude that gives a privileged position to the literature that records active participation in combat also encourages women writers to exclude themselves from serious consideration. The vigor of the following commitment—"There are moments when I feel that every one of us—women and children as well as men—ought to be marching out towards that battle-line— if only to die there"—is quickly deflated: "I am laughing while I write that sentence, for I have a vision of myself limping along, carrying a gun in *both* hands—I could not lift it with one—and falling down, and having to be carefully stood up again. We mere lookers-on encumber the earth at this epoch."[6]

It will be the object of this chapter to challenge the assumption that women's writing about their wartime experiences is in any way less authentic than men's. The subjects they write about are, of necessity, different, but it will be argued that the impact of the war resonates through their work just as profoundly.

It is important to emphasize the fact that the war deeply affected both men and women. Women's experiences during the war were significant and long lasting, and their realization in writing constitutes an important chronicle of change, self-realization, and literary experiment. What they did not experience is *combat,* the description of which is the central omission from women's writing and which, when it does occur, is often poor stuff. It is important not to be misled by such apparently reasonable statements as the following: "When women have *imagined* war itself, however, it has frequently been in abstract, stereotypical tropes that bear little relation to war's realities. . . . [Their writing has ranged] from patriotic doggerel . . . to First World War jingoist women poets *imagining* the Western front as a place of freedom" (emphasis added).[7] The war does not equate only to the western front. It encompasses ambulance driving; death in accidents in munitions factories; the privations suffered on the home front, in the occupied territories, and in Germany itself; the sinking of the Lusitania; medical attention offered under fire; the war in Serbia; aerial bombardment; the pain of bereavement. A million and one horrors occurred elsewhere than on the western front, and they were directly experienced, not imagined, by women. And this partial catalog avoids mention of the profound social and cultural changes that occurred during, after, and because of the war. It is not a technical or semantic point to object to the conflation of war and combat, because it is one of the major reasons why women's war writing has been ignored.

American journalist Mildred Aldrich lived in the village of Huiry on the banks of the Marne throughout the war, and her four books of letters written during those years were extremely popular at the time. A comparison of two passages from her letter of 5 December 1914 is revealing. On a visit to the battlefield she sees a house:

> a shell, its walls alone standing. As its windows and doors had been blown out, we could look in from the street to the interior of what

had evidently been a comfortable country house. It was now like an uncovered box, in the centre of which there was a conical shaped heap of ashes as high as the top of the fireplace. We could see where the stairs had been, but its entire contents had been burned down to a heap of ashes—burned as thoroughly as wood in a fireplace. I could not have believed in such absolute destruction if I had not seen it.

While we were gazing at the wreck I noticed an old woman leaning against the wall and watching us. Out of her weather beaten, time furrowed old face looked a pair of dark eyes, red rimmed and blurred with much weeping. She was rubbing her distorted old hands together nervously. . . . [I discovered] this wreck had been, for years, her home, that she had lived there all alone, and that everything she had in the world—her furniture, her clothing, and her *savings*—had been burned in the house.

You can hardly understand that unless you know these people. They keep their savings hidden.

Aldrich's ability to understand and record in telling detail the domestic effects of war on civilian survivors rests securely on the confident knowledge of someone who has lived a similar life. She knows the height of a fireplace, where the stairs would be, how wood burns; she knows the people and understands the physical distortions caused by age and hard work; she knows the rural distrust of the banking system.

Later, she comes upon a scene of carnage:

First the graves were scattered, for the boys lie buried just where they fell—cradled in the bosom of the mother country that nourished them, and for whose safety they laid down their lives. As we advanced they became more numerous, until we reached a point where, as far as we could see, in every direction, floated the little *tricolore* flags, like fine flowers in the landscape. They made tiny spots against the far-off horizon line, and groups like beds of flowers in the foreground, and we knew that, behind the skyline, there were more.

Here and there was a haystack with one grave beside it, and again there would be one, usually partly burned, almost encircled with the tiny flags which said: "Here sleep the heroes."

It was a disturbing and a thrilling sight. . . . It seemed to me a fine thing to lie out there in the open, in the soil of the fields their simple death has made holy, the duty well done, the dread over, each one just where he fell defending his mother-land, enshrined forever in the loving memory of the land he had saved, in graves to be watered for years, not only by the tears of those near and dear to them, but by those of the heirs to their glory—the children of the coming generation of free France.[8]

This second passage reveals only too clearly Aldrich's inability to realize what death in combat entails as she reverts to the sentimental and clichéd language of patriotism in an attempt to express it: "boys . . . fell . . . cradled in the bosom of the mother country that nourished them . . . laid down their lives . . . 'Here sleep the heroes' . . . a fine thing to lie out there in the open . . . their simple death . . . holy . . . fell . . . mother-land, enshrined . . . heirs to their glory." The abstract nouns with which this passage is loaded stand in direct contrast to the factual details of the first extract. That her use of flowers signals a further avoidance of reality is signified by the insubstantial nature of the verb she uses: the flags "*floated* . . . like fine flowers in the landscape . . . like beds of flowers" (emphasis added). Of women war poets' similar use of floral imagery, Janet Montefiore writes: "It is as if the existence of mutilated and dead bodies cannot be named directly. . . . [there is] a conscious articulation of denial. . . . using the tradition of pastoral in order at once to name and to deny death." These are, she concludes, "[f]lowery evasions."[9] The poverty of the second passage should not, however, blind us to the poignant precision of the first.

Barbara Baer is correct when she writes that women "tend to ignore weapons and . . . leave out description of war itself."[10] It is well nigh impossible to find any extended description of men on active combat at the front; or on the nature of trench warfare, gas and bayonets; or their effect on the soldiers. In one of the very rare stories to show women "in action," American writer Mary Roberts Rinehart is able to maintain a humorous tone by putting the blame for any injury or death that may occur onto the enemy itself:

> Well, the attack started just then and Aggie and I got our revolvers and began shooting as rapidly as possible, firing from the end of the village, and with Mr. Burton's grenades from one side and our revolvers from the other it made a tremendous noise. Aggie and I did our best, I know, to appear to be a large number, firing and then moving to a new point and firing again. I must say from the way those Germans ran toward their own lines . . . I was not surprised at the rapidity of the final retreat which ended the war. As Aggie said later, we were not there to kill them unless necessary, but they ran so fast at times it was difficult to avoid hitting them. They fairly ran into the bullets.[11]

A closer look at the manner in which Rinehart writes of weapons and war is revealing. The use of generalized terms allows her to further absolve her characters from any direct responsibility: "attack . . . revolvers . . . shooting . . . firing . . . grenades . . . revolvers . . . tremendous noise . . . firing . . . moving . . . firing . . . ran . . . retreat . . . ran . . . hitting . . . ran . . . bullets." While not employing the sentimental abstractions of the passage from Aldrich quoted above, this is a nonspecific and nontechnical manner of writing about weapons and war that declares the author's and the characters' ignorance— and thus innocence—of them.

Unusually, Bessie Marchant's undemanding spy story, *A Girl Munition Worker*, shows the heroine, Deborah Lynch, not only shooting at but wounding an enemy spy. This action is of little importance militarily, however, having more significance as part of the thematic relationship between the heroine and the hero, Dick Ferris. They both begin doing the same war work—making tents for the troops; the comparison of their respective contributions to the war effort continues when he enlists and she takes up work in a munitions factory. Just before the shooting incident occurs, he is still safely in England, on sentry duty at the factory where she is working, more dangerously, with cordite. Furthermore, Deborah shoots the German spy, using Dick's rifle. The temporary reversal of positions encapsulated in her assuming his role as a combatant may have served to emphasize the importance of women's war work, but gender roles are speedily normalized and traditional standards reasserted: we learn that he has failed in his proper role by virtue of being drugged, while she immediately reverts to hers by fainting once the gun has been discharged.

More typical of women writers' depiction of warfare is Willa Cather. In *One of Ours,* a novel of more than 450 pages, the traditional events and scenery of war fiction account for no more than a dozen: the first account of battle quickly moves to and stays with the wounded hero, Claude Wheeler; the final action, which includes the German offensive on the American lines, ends in his death.[12]

At least Claude Wheeler is, however briefly, a soldier. More often, when women writers do describe battle, they employ as mouthpieces heroes who have a medical role or are relatives of men at the front: in other words, men who are fulfilling what has traditionally been the function of women. Claude Wheeler himself is depicted in the role of nurse during an outbreak of influenza on the transport ship taking him to France; "Book Four: The Voyage of the Anchises" (264–319) is longer than the sections in which he is a combatant. Similarly, in "Vignettes from Life at the Rear," Dorothy Canfield puts the description of the front into the mouths of men who are a stretcher bearer and a despatch carrier.[13]

Claire Tylee links this practice to women's definition of themselves as nonmilitants. "Since war inextricably involves the intentional killing and harming of other people, it is significant that these women [writers] do not imagine destruction from the point of view of the destroyer, but as passive sufferers or compassionate helpers of the victims. They can sympathise with pain and grief, which are the dominant emotions of all these novels. But never with the 'savage war-cry' of jubilant slaughter. . . . It remained fundamental to the Englishwoman's conception of herself that women did not kill."[14] But this seems to be at best a partial explanation. The deployment of men in traditional women's roles may reflect women's inability or refusal to imagine the point of view of the destroyer, and it may also be a strategy for authenticating women's writing about combat, but these explanations do not account for the fact that the blurring of traditional gender roles also occurs in writing about the home front.

Despite its title, Edith Wharton's *A Son at the Front* is set in Paris, not at the front, and thus the only roles available to the protagonists are those traditionally assigned to women—"the chorus of the tragedy."[15] The central character, Campton, a father scheming to keep his son from returning to the front, identifies himself with women: "They blamed women who were cowards about their husbands. . . . Well—he was as bad as any one of them."[16] Campton is not only forced into assuming a woman's role, but the role itself is disparaged: "chorus . . . blamed . . . cowards . . . bad." In her memoir *Testament of Youth,* Vera Brittain captures the identical tone: ". . . all that was required of women was to go home and keep quiet. . . . I felt miserably conscious that, apart from the demand for doctors and nurses, women in war seemed to be at a discount except as the appendages of soldiers."[17] But while Campton has to accept that he has been relegated to the unglamorous role of noncombatant, Brittain will come to insist that she has an important role to play in the war as a woman. It would appear that the accentuation of gender roles that occurred during the war had the unthought-of consequence of encouraging women to question their validity and to keep the issue at the center of their writing.

Women's Traditional Concerns

While what women did *not* write about can thus be seen to have its own significance, the topics women did write about during the war were the predictable ones of the home, childbirth and childcare, and nursing. Traditionally, the private sphere of the home was women's personal and literary forte, and this translated in wartime into an obsession with domestic conditions, typically food, housekeeping, and deprivation. Mildred Aldrich recounts, at different times, that it "is over a fortnight since we had sugar or butter or coffee. . . . I have managed to get a little coal. . . . The temperature of the rest of the house is down almost to zero . . . it is very damp, as it rains continually. . . . my coal gave out in February. . . . There is no coal in sight. . . . Our food problem is going to be a hard one. . . . Milk is almost nonexistent. We have . . . no butter, almost no coffee, no cereals of any sort, no fruit. . . . [The children] are being largely nourished on potatoes."[18]

Food, hunger, and marketing also dominate Dorothy Canfield's story "On the Edge"; its title actually refers to the strains on the heroine's mental health, but by conjuring up the ghost of the phrase "on the edge of the war zone," it suggests that her suffering is a version of war service. It is a story that focuses on the role of the wartime mother who suffers the constant "fatigue of preparing and serving the lunch for the six noisy children, always too hungry for the small portions, so that at the last she divided most of her own part among them. . . . she strove desperately to keep the little ones cheerful and occupied and at the same time to mend and bake and darn and clean and iron and carry ashes out and coal in."[19]

The passage below describes which foods are available, the dramatic rise in prices, the effect on the children, and the common fellowship between two mothers. One, Jeanne Bruneau,

> priced the cauliflowers, sighed, and bought potatoes, and less of them than she had hoped to have, the price having gone up again. She was horrified to find that rice cost more than it had, an impossible sum per pound, even the broken, poor-quality grade. She would try macaroni as a substitute. There *was* no macaroni, the woman clerk informed her. . . . Well, perhaps she might be able to manage prunes. . . . "Prunes, Madame Bruneau? They are only for the rich." She named a price which made Jeanne gasp.
> She calculated the amount she would need for one portion each for her big family. It was out of the question. . . . She appealed desperately to the woman clerk, "What do *you* do?" she asked. "We do without," answered the other woman briefly.
> "But your children? Growing children can't be in good health without *some* fruit."
> "They're not in good health," answered the other grimly. "My Marthe has eczema, and the doctor says that Henri is just ripe for tuberculosis." Her voice died. . . .
> Then they both drew a long breath and began to add up together the cost of Jeanne's purchases. . . .
> If she could only leave [the children] at home, could only spare them that daily ordeal of the visit to the bakeshop where their poor little heads were turned at the sight and odor of all that food. Not to have *bread* to give them![20]

Although one is selling and the other buying, it is clear that when "they *both* drew a long breath and began to add up *together* the cost of Jeanne's purchases" the women's roles as carers have become more important than their positions on opposite sides of the counter.

Childbirth, too, is a recurrent theme in women's wartime writing. It is central to Canfield's "La Pharmacienne," in which Madeleine gives birth "alone, pitted against a malign universe, which wished to injure her baby. . . . [Later she] stood there in that abomination of desolation, with death all around . . . looking down at the baby, and smiling."[21] But the contrast between men's destruction and women's creativity implicit in such juxtapositions is also seen to have implications for the future. As Dr. Prince says of an expectant mother in E. M. Delafield's *The War-Workers,* " 'She's probably going to be of more use to the nation, let me tell you, than all the rest of you put together' "[22] (the comment is particularly sharp in being addressed to women war workers). Other writers take up the same theme. After the war women must:

> be ready to repopulate right. After the battles are won and man's work of conquest is done, woman's war work will only have begun. . . . every one of these men once was builded with such exquisite art and

such infinite labour and such toilsome pain and anguish by God and a woman! It is a stupendous task of creation to be done over again when the armies shall have finished their work. Bone of her bone and flesh of her flesh, God and woman must rebuild the race. . . .

Not a captain of industry who assembles the engines of war, not a general who directs the armies, may do for his country what you can do who stand beside its cradles. The cry that rings out over Empires bleeding in the throes of death is the oldest cry in the world. Women wanted for maternity![23]

Women writers took the opportunity to suggest that the traditional peacetime roles women continued to perform during the war had gained an additional resonance. Nurture and care were seen to extend from family concerns to the land itself. I have written elsewhere about the frequency with which American women writers commented on the special connection they perceived between women and their wartime work on the land.[24] This was especially true in their descriptions of French farming, which was carried out almost exclusively by women. It can be summed up in the comment of an American singer who spent six months traveling around France entertaining the troops: "The country is cultivated to the last inch—and all done by the women."[25] The phenomenon extended also to English writers commenting on French women's assumption of agricultural responsibilities and the work of Land Girls in England. This was more than simple objective reporting: the symbolic dissonance of women having the physical freedom to work the land in men's places, during a war in which men had literally to dig themselves into the earth, cannot have been lost on either men or women.

The emphasis women writers place on nurture, childcare, and birth extends more widely, and most examples manifest equally explicit role contrasts. Edith Wharton notes that in a general's study, "it was amusingly incongruous to see the sturdy provincial furniture littered with war-maps, trench plans, aeroplane photographs and all the documentation of modern war [while through] the windows bees hummed, the garden rustled, and one felt, close by, behind the walls of other gardens, the untroubled continuance of a placid and orderly bourgeois life."[26]

Other women writers also commend their heroines for creating order, for establishing stability—"a placid and orderly bourgeois life"—out of chaos. Dorothy Canfield combines the recurrent motifs of order and childcare when she describes how Paulette Nidart "tried to set to order their little corner saved from chaos . . . putting back . . . arranging neatly . . . smoothing out the blankets . . . washing the faces and hands of the children."[27]

Of course, women wrote about nursing during the war; the subject is amply illustrated in book after book, both fiction and memoir,[28] and in a manner that refutes the criticism that women could not deal with the horrors of war. These accounts convey the authors' knowledge of the effects of gas, shelling, and disease and their ability to express in graphic detail the physical gruesomeness of war and the emotions to which it gives rise. Gertrude Atherton summarizes the activities of the women who have given up "every waking hour to ameliorating the lot of the defenders of their hearth and their honor, or nursing the wounded in hospital, [women who] have been stark up against the physical side: whether making bombs in factories, bandages or uniforms, washing gaping wounds, preparing shattered bodies for burial, or listening to the horrid tales of men and women home on leave."[29]

And they write too about what they fear will be a lifetime of nursing after the war:

> Nothing about here was broken but men—and women were mending them!
>   At length they had the sergeant patched up as well as they could. He would never again work at his skilled trade. But . . . they sent him back to his wife in the north of England. . . .
>   "Discharged from the service," his papers read. But his wife will never be! . . . These are the women whom not even the Peace Treaty will discharge from their "national service." Every Great Push makes more of them. . . . Who shall say whether she too may be conscripted to "carry on" for life? For this is the way of war with women.[30]

The military imagery used in connection with women's activities in this extract ("discharged . . . 'national service' . . . conscripted to 'carry on'") is not atypical. It occurs in fiction, as when Jeanne Bruneau almost breaks down under the pressures of malnutrition and worry about children and husband, and likens the experience to being "like men after too long shell fire when they walk dazedly straight into danger."[31] It is there in *Testament of Youth,* when Vera Brittain unconsciously evokes a military comparison to illustrate her early nursing experiences: ". . . I never completely overcame the aching of my back and the soreness of my feet throughout the time that I worked there, and felt perpetually as if I had just returned from a series of long route marches."[32] And we find it in documentary works, too; in *Mobilizing Women-Power,* Harriet Stanton Blatch wrote that by compelling women to work, the war sent them "over the top . . . up the scaling-ladder, and out into 'All Man's Land.' "[33]

The figurative conflation of women's and men's war work can be even more direct and personal: in Mary Borden's sketch, "Blind," the nurses have become the combatants: "This is the second battlefield. The battle now is going on over the helpless bodies of these men. It is we who are doing the fighting now, with their real enemies."[34] Mildred Aldrich, still writing of domestic privations in *The Peak of the Load,* compares her plight with that of the soldiers in the trenches: "I am almost as cold as the boys out there in the rain and the mud."[35] And even the timid Nelly of Mrs. Humphry Ward's novel, *"Missing,"* comes eventually to recognize her worth and strength in terms of men's training: "I thought the first weeks that I was in hospital, I *must* break down. I never dreamt that anyone could feel so tired—so deadly ill—and yet go on. And then one began, little by little, to get hardened,—of course, I'm only now beginning to feel that!—and it seems like being born again, with a quite new body, that one can make—yes, *make*—do as one likes. That's what the soldiers tell me—about *their* training. And they wonder at it, as I do."[36]

Women writers compare their war experiences with those of men in other ways, too, when they write about the work women undertake. Typical is Mabel Daggett, who reveals a detailed knowledge of local domestic arrangements and implications equal to that of Mildred Aldrich when she writes of Madeleine Danau, who

> was only fourteen years old at the time her father, the baker, was mobilized. A baker in France . . . is a most necessary functionary in the community, for as everybody has for years bought bread, nobody even knows how to make it at home any more. The whole neighbouring countryside . . . was most dependent on the baker, and the baker was gone away to war. It was then that Madeleine proved equal to doing the duty that was nearest to her. She promptly stepped into her father's place before the bread-trough and the oven. She gets up each morning at four o'clock, and with the aid of her little brother, a year younger than herself, she makes each day 800 lb. of bread, which is delivered in a cart by another brother and sister. The radius of the district is some ten miles, and no household since war began has missed its daily supply of bread.[37]

This assumption of men's work occurred, and was commented on, in all the warring countries. In Berlin, wrote Josephine Therese, "women are everywhere, performing all kinds of menial occupations, from which the men of the lower classes have been taken to swell the ranks of the army. They collect the garbage; they deliver ice and merchandise from the stores . . . ; they work in the stores, of course; run elevators; and act as conductresses and subway guards—the latter wearing most unbecoming bloomers, reaching to the knees, and thick stockings. Finally they wield pick and shovel on the streets."[38]

The very title of Dorothy Canfield's "La Pharmacienne" identifies the woman with the occupation she assumes when her husband goes to war.[39] This is another story that deals with women's role in restoring order and stability; but significantly, this time, once the Germans have retreated from the village, the restoration of the workplace comes before that of the home. Such changes of priority may not bode well for men in future. Gertrude Atherton comments on the physical benefits to women of their labor in the munitions factories: "As I looked at those bare heavily muscled arms I wondered if any man belonging to them would ever dare say his soul was his own again. . . . [the women's] bare muscular arms looked quite capable of laying a man prostrate if he came home and ordered them about, and their character and pride had developed in proportion."[40]

The comparison with men can extend to a claim for complete equality of experience. Willa Cather says, of all the women waiting for news at home, that "for these women the war was . . . life, and everything that went into it. To be alive, to be conscious and have one's faculties, was to be in the war."[41] Deborah Lynch, the girl munition worker, "looked upon her overalls as a uniform . . . she would henceforth walk with death as closely as her soldier father. She, too, belonged to the British Army now. . . . 'If death must come, let us pray that it may find us doing our bit, for we are soldiers of the King.' "[42]

My last illustrations were selected from imaginatively created fiction, but similar comments occur in documentary accounts. Mairi Chisholm and the Baroness T'Serclaes, famous during the war for running the most forward of the nursing posts, endured constant privation. In cutting off their hair, they minimized the infestation of head lice from which they suffered, but, more important, they consciously underwent a ritual laden with spiritual and psychological significance, thus thrusting "away all idea of fears, nerves, or feminine weaknesses." In cutting off their hair they became men: " 'With that little bundle of hair went all our nervousnesses, all our fears of rats, our dislike of dirty food, and our ideas of home comforts. We became soldiers from that hour.' "[43]

Such comparisons extended beyond seeing women as soldiers to claiming them as casualties of the war. They not only took part in the war but died in it, too: "The war killed Christine, just as surely as if she had been a soldier in the trenches."[44] Mabel Daggett draws attention to those women who have died or been wounded in the war:

> it is no surprise to come on women's names in any of the lists, "Dead," "Wounded," or "Decorated." The French Academy out of seventy prizes in 1916 awarded no less than forty-seven to women "as most distinguished examples of military courage." Among these the Croix de Guerre has been given to Madame Macherez, capable citizeness of Soissons, who has been daily at the Mairie in an executive capacity, and to Mll Sellier, who has been in charge of the Red Cross hospital there during the long months of the bombardment. The Cross of the Legion of Honour along with the Cross of Christ decorates the front of the black habit of Sister Julie, the nun of Gerbéviller who held the invading Germans at bay while she stood guard over the wounded French soldiers at her improvised hospital. It's like this in all of the warring countries.[45]

Women writers give details of women civilians who remained near the front: they " 'oughtn't to be here,' our guide explained; 'but about a hundred and fifty begged so hard to stay that the General gave them leave' "; Wharton also commends others who have bravely continued working through enemy attacks.[46] Other writers draw attention to individual women whose activities they admire. Dorothy Canfield, for example, in "France's Fighting Woman Doctor," writes of Dr. Nicole Girard-Mangin, "the woman doctor who was mobilized and sent to the front by mistake, and who proved herself so fearless and useful that she was kept there for two years, amid bursting shells and rattling mitrailleuses."[47]

The comparison of their situation with that of men extends in some women writers to perceiving their agony as indivisible from the anguish of men. For Mary Hamilton's heroine, "the war still went on, Harold was still in France, more men—men she knew, as well as thousands she didn't— were killed or maimed, and there seemed no end to it, her own pain, repeated on every side, became part of a universal pattern, and she felt they had fallen into Hell together, and there was no past and no future for any of them. War had submerged life: other activities than those dedicated to it had ceased."[48] Others claim that women empathetically share men's physical pain. Antonia White writes of Clara Batchelor, whose insanity is at least partially caused by the war. In her madness she "went through a new agony. She became the dead boy. She spoke with his voice. She felt the pain of amputated limbs, of blinded eyes. She coughed up blood from lungs torn to rags by shrapnel. Over and over again, in trenches, in field hospitals, in German camps, she died a lingering death."[49]

It is not just sophisticated or feminist writers who make these points. We may not be surprised that Edith Wharton should write of Mariette, who cannot return from the front to the relative safety of Paris, and of a woman and child who disappear during the occupation while the father of the family is safe in Paris guarding a bridge; nor do we wonder that she should describe the women in such a way as to suggest a comparison with men experiencing the danger of being at the front: "no word came from her or the child. They . . . were in an occupied province [but Mme. Lebel] . . . continued to have fairly frequent reassuring news" of her menfolk.[50] But the more prosaic Dorothy Canfield also offers a reversal of roles in the story of "le soldat Deschamps," whose wife is behind enemy lines while he is safe at the rear.[51] Even the conservative Meriel Buchanan makes similar implicit claims; on more than one occasion after a description of the suffering of Russian soldiers we are immediately reminded of the suffering of refugees, with a significant emphasis on the plight of women. They include "a small baby whose mother had died or been lost on the way . . . a women distraught and wild seeking everywhere for a little girl of three years old whose fate no-one knew . . . long lines of patient women waiting through slush and snow and bitter cold for bread and milk and meat."[52]

By assuming equal pain, equal suffering, women writers magnify their role in the war. A more significant aspect of this reversal, however, lies in its implicit *reduction* of men's role. Thus we see that while men's war writing give priority to their experience of combat, women's war writing deploys their traditional concerns to examine gender roles and to make implicitly subversive claims for the significance of their own experiences. Judith Sensibar, writing specifically of *A Son at the Front,* claims that Wharton "anticipated feminist critics of the late twentieth century by asking how the social disruptions of the Great War reveal and affect socially constructed notions of masculinity and femininity." She argues that the novel contains "much that had not been the subject of fiction . . . writes a different war, a war behind the lines and a war within that . . . will continue as long as masculine, homophobic gender classifications are in place."[53] While this is a perceptive comment on Wharton, it is also far more widely applicable. The war made women more alert to contemporary gender systems, and their views on them and their inherent inequality were widely, if not always explicitly, expressed.

But such a subject does not inevitably distinguish between men's and women's writing. Any consideration of the writing of the war years may well come to the conclusion that both men and women were struggling to understand the social and gender roles that had been imposed on them. A careful analysis of subject matter uncovers real and deep similarities between men's and women's wartime writing, similarities that are possible because both employ the first-person narrative—the narrator as participant, a subject considered at greater length in chapter 5. Setting aside until then the full significance of the first-person narrative, and despite the apparent differences of subject we have noted so far, it is possible to arrive at a synopsis of characteristics common to wartime narratives that underscores the narrator's experiences, whatever his or her sex. It might be something like this: usually rich in descriptive details, such accounts recount the spiritual education of individuals or groups as they progress through stages of exposure to the war. Beginning with recruitment and training, the journey to the front and initial shocking experiences, there then follows, usually horrifyingly, the appearance of the dead, injury, hospitals and nursing; the struggle to survive and to save. In almost all cases the continuity and repetitiveness of each individual's experience lead to disillusionment and a new sense of what the future must hold, or what social changes must be achieved to permit a better future.[54]

One novel that partakes of all these characteristics is *"Not So Quiet . . ." Stepdaughters of War,* written by Evadne Price under the pseudonym Helen Zenna Smith. It graphically recounts the experiences of Helen Z. Smith, an ambulance driver at the front.[55] The events of the novel conform very closely to the pattern described above. Moreover, as Brian Murdoch points out, the novel "contains a variety of specific motifs familiar in other anti war writing,"[56] in particular the conflict between the generations and the contrast between the opinions and values prevalent at home and the realities of the front. Murdoch writes that the "value of the novel . . . lies in its uncompromising *engagement,* and by the sustaining of three independent major motifs: first, that of the collapse of the code of behaviour imposed upon young women; secondly, that of an all-embracing loathing, and more importantly a fear of the war . . . and thirdly the motif of the lost generation itself, and the contrast between the young, who are involved in the war, and their parents in particular, who blackmail and gloat."[57] He could have added the extreme disillusionment, the all-pervasive cynicism that came to characterize an entire generation.

In the novel's sequel, *Women of the Aftermath*, the heroine recalls how women:

> responded to the call, sentimental, noble, sloppy, doing-our-bit, all uplifted, patriotic, and unpowdered, that's how we went into the war—but we emerged a bit different to what people expected. . . . We were bullied and browbeaten and frozen and starved. We wallowed in slime and blood and mud. We learnt to drink and curse and blaspheme with the worst of you. . . . Laugh and shout, wave your Union jack, peace has come at last, what does it matter about women like me, now the killing is done? Sheltered young women like me who walked straight from suburbia into hell—one week-end having tea with the Vicar's wife . . . the next week-end all alone with an ambulance of raving, blaspheming, pain-crazed, dying men.[58]

Here the author compares what was seen as typical of women before the war with how they emerged from it. The postwar women are compared with "the worst of you," that is, the worst of men. What brought about their transformation is summed up in three words: "slime and blood and mud," perceived by many to have been the sole province of men.

Writing by women who supported the war also shares something with men's prowar writing. It should not be forgotten that in Britain the war was initially welcomed and fought by a volunteer army. Many women assumed a similarly simple patriotic stance and wrote prowar tracts, and not all of them were unthinking. May Sinclair's novel *The Tree of Heaven* is a case in point: it is critical of the suffrage movement and sees the war as a cause of genuine and commendable community and cooperation. It also includes a woman's explicit desire to be a man: "Safety was hard and bitter to her. Her hidden self was unsatisfied; it had a monstrous longing. It wanted to go where the guns sounded and the shells burst, and the villages flamed and smoked; to go along the straight, flat roads between the poplars where the refugees had gone, so that her nerves and flesh should know and feel their suffering and their danger. She was not feeling anything now except the shame of her immunity."[59]

We have seen that those writings about women's wartime experiences that rely on their authenticity offer a gender-specific parallel to the classics of men's war writing. An underlying conformity to an extrapolated abstract of war writing underpins yet other women's writing. But the predominance of these two modes should not blind us to a third. By a closer examination of the passage from *The Tree of Heaven* we can begin to identify the nontraditional subjects women wrote about, the hidden subjects that constitute a different history, a different agenda from men's. It was not something women writers found easy to address. Notice in the passage how it is a "hidden self" that is unsatisfied; the longing she feels is described as "monstrous" and has to be referred to more often with a neutral "it" before it can be acknowledged that it is "*her* nerves and flesh" that are involved.

= A Different Agenda =

The desire to share the burden of the war in full comes from many quarters. Letters from the trenches, Vera Brittain wrote to her brother, "made me wish desperately that I were a man and could train myself to play the 'Great Game with Death'—I wish it were *my* obvious duty to 'go and live in a ditch,' as Roland called it."[60] Similarly, Rose Macaulay's heroine wails: "Oh I do so want to go and fight. . . . I want to go and help to end it. . . . Oh, it's rotten not being able to; simply rotten. . . . Why *shouldn't* girls?"[61] And Temple Bailey's Jean "had yearned to be a man that she might stand in the forefront of battle. She had envied the women of Russia who had formed a Battalion of Death."[62]

It is not hard to discern, behind this traditional patriotic stance, a more radical dislike of women's traditional role. Note the emphatic emotional "indeed" in the following extract from another letter of Vera Brittain, this time to Roland Leighton: "I am quite sure that had I been a boy I should have gone off to take part in it long ago; indeed I have wasted many moments regretting that I am a girl. Women get all the dreariness of war and none of its exhilaration. . . . The fact that circumstances are abnormal is not consolation for being unable to take active part in them."[63]

It is hardly surprising that Mary Roberts Rinehart's redoubtable heroine Tish, one of the few women characters depicted leading an attack on the German lines, should "regret that she was a woman."[64] It may be more significant that, while Lady Londonderry criticizes the "martial spirits of the Women's Volunteer Reserve," she accepts that "their intentions were of the best—it was a hard and cruel fate that had created them women."[65]

Olive Dent argues that it is not enough for women to accept the old roles. Reflecting on Charles Kingsley's "For men must work, and women must weep," she comments, "True enough, the women would weep, and weep in full measure, but that was no reason for an apathetic acceptance. Meantime there was surely work to be done."[66] The contrast between the two sentences—between the archaic "weep" and the modern "work," between the subjunctive "would" and the active "done"—sums up the conflict between the two perceptions of women's function.

To some the contrast between the perceived roles was a simple and inevitable result of wartime experience: "these Sisters and nurses of the front have seen sights to dry up the last drop of sentimental pity."[67] But it is interesting to note how quickly, and among what conventional women, domestic roles were also challenged, even for those who did not experience war's horrors. Helen Davenport Gibbons's memoir, *A Little Gray Home in France,* recounts her experiences offering what comforts her home could provide to serving fellow Americans. The book contains no evidence whatsoever that she herself was other than happy with her role as wife and mother, but her experiences set her thinking. When she dines at an American mess, she writes, "I reflected that neatness and precision in preparing and serving food belong not to women alone," and she reckons that if women would take up active war work they "would know they had a better job than knitting."[68] Indeed, there is evidence that one of the elements of German Kultur that some women held responsible for the war was its relegation of women to merely domestic roles.[69]

It was often the traditional feminine virtues that the war was thought to change: Mrs. Humphry Ward writes of Nelly, who "had been an old-fashioned, simple girl, brought up in a backwater of life. Now she was being drawn into that world of the new woman—where are women policemen, and women chauffeurs, and militant suffragists, and women in overalls and breeches, and many other strange types. The war has shown us—suddenly and marvellously—the adaptability of women. Would little Nelly, too, prove as plastic as the rest, and in the excitement of meeting new demands, and reaching out to new powers, forget the old needs and sweetnesses?"[70]

If war acts as a stimulus to make women openly reconsider their roles and to write about that reconsideration, it also makes them reconsider what they have been told are their inherent natures, and to write about that, too. The *hidden* topic for women writers is not the challenge to their social roles, which the war encouraged them to make, but the challenge to the deeper identity they had been allocated by society. If the old sweetnesses disappeared, different strengths would take their place, and perhaps they were equally inherent, merely unused before the war. As Gertrude Atherton wrote, thousands of women "have developed unsuspected capacities, energies, endurance, above all genuine executive abilities . . . never before have women done as much thinking for themselves as they are doing today . . . in the instance of war, the passion of usefulness, the sense of dedication to a high cause, the necessary frequent suppression of self, stamp the soul with an impress that never can be obliterated."[71]

This profound change had postwar implications. When the soldier returns to his wife, wrote Mabel Daggett, "he will hold her off, so, at arm's length, and look long into her eyes and deep into her soul. And lo, he shall see there the New Woman. This is not the woman whom he left behind when he marched away to the Great World War. Something profound has happened to her since. It is woman's coming of age. Look, she is turning the ring on her finger to-day."[72]

It was not to be expected that most women would experience the liberation that the war brought to some with the insouciance of Mabel Daggett, but it brought some women a freedom that came from work and independence. No doubt some women did welcome "the war as a chance to break away from their social origins."[73]

One of the threats to women's ability and freedom to undertake war duties came from their families, and here, too, women began to question the familial identity that encompassed them. When they write about morale on the home front, how their families seem unable to cope, cannot comprehend their experiences nor how important they are to the war effort, they sound a characteristic note of the times that is not confined to women—though perhaps they express it with less bitterness than men. When Vera Brittain comments that the ". . . despondency at home was certainly making many of us in France quite alarmed," she might have been a man writing. She continues, however, by expressing her deeper fear that for no other reason than that she was a woman, she may be recalled to home duties: "because we were women we feared perpetually that, just as our work was reaching its climax, our families would need our youth and vitality for their own support. One of my cousins . . . had already been summoned home from her canteen work in Boulogne; she was only one of many, for as the War continued to wear out strength and spirits, the middle-aged generation, having irrevocably yielded up its sons, began to lean with increasing weight upon its daughters."[74]

Thus the choice between incompatible claims with which women have always been tormented was seen to take a particularly desperate wartime form: "What exhausts women in wartime is not the strenuous and unfamiliar tasks that fall upon them, nor even the hourly dread of death for husbands or lovers or brothers or sons; it is the incessant conflict between personal and national claims which wears out their energy and breaks their spirit."[75]

Bessie Marchant's *A Girl Munition Worker* is by no means as conscious a consideration of conflicting "personal and national" responsibilities as Brittain's *Testament of Youth* or E. M. Delafield's *The War-Workers*. It is for that very reason that we should recognize the significance of its dramatization of the conflict women experienced between domestic and patriotic duties, between an imposed and an adopted identity. Marchant's heroine Deborah begins by dividing her time equally between war work and domestic chores, although she wishes to devote herself fully to the war effort: the "division of labour was a piece of real self sacrifice."[76] Her ambition is not understood, and when she does achieve her goal of working in a munitions factory, her Aunt Agatha finds what she regards as Deborah's desertion quite unacceptable, and writes "a really pathetic letter concerning the uncalled for character of the sacrifice she was making."[77] Eventually, in the continuing contrast of commitment and danger that the book dramatizes, Dick goes to the front, and Deborah becomes the leader of the workers; although women's war work on the home front is thus directly compared with and found equal to men's work, it is only the woman who must fulfill her domestic responsibilities first.

Although wartime work was demanding and perhaps demeaning, some books argue that it empowered workers: Marielle in Atherton's *The White Morning* says: " 'Think of the freedom of being a Red Cross nurse, and all the men at the front.' "[78] And Wharton's Campton has to recognize that just as he is restricted by his inactivity during the war, women may be liberated by their work: "Was it possible she had found her vocation? . . . [She was] as absorbed in her work as if it had been a long thwarted vocation."[79] Although it is important that this element in women's writing be neither misunderstood nor overestimated, there *were* women for whom wartime freedom gave rise to feelings of exhilaration at what Elshtain calls "a great transformative experience."[80] Mabel Daggett may be unique in the outspoken clarity with which she comments on the women who responded to the call for workers—"Every time a man drops dead in the trenches, a woman steps permanently into the niche he used to hold in industry, in commerce, in the professions, in world affairs. . . . Really it was like taking the last trench in the Great Push when the women's battalions arrived at Lombard and Threadneedle Streets"[81]— but she was only stating openly what was secretly being thought by a number of men and women at the time. Sandra Gilbert, writing of "the excitement of war," claims that "the exhilaration (along with the anxiety) of [wartime freedom and power] is as dramatically rendered in wartime poems, stories, and memoirs by women as are the very different responses to the war in usually better known works by men."[82]

Some of the more outspoken feminist writers went even further than Daggett. They found nothing to fear in a sexual disjunction, did not worry about a "barrier of experience" inhibiting communications between the sexes, were unconcerned about being rejected by men, and admitted no guilt. *The White Morning* begins with a rejection of marriage: the reasons why the three Niebuhr sisters "solemnly pledged one another never to marry"[83] arise from their father's authoritarian behavior, which in turn comes directly from his military character; from their mother's experience of marriage, which is dismissed as "thirty unspeakable years"[84]; and from their sister Marielle's life as an officer's wife. Nor are they alone in their criticism of men. Their friend Heloise is even more explicit: " 'God! How I hate men! . . . Sick or well, German, English, French, I loathe them all alike. Obscene beasts every one of them.' "[85]

But while these are its most extreme examples, the novel sees similar feelings extending nationally and charts "the growing rebellion of German women" who are "restless and dissatisfied" and who experience a "developing sense of revolt against the attitude of the German male to the sex of the mother that bore him . . . the deep slow secret revolt against the insolent and inconsiderate attitude of the German male that had been growing among its women for some fifteen years before the outbreak of the war . . . thousands of [women] were muttering to one another."[86]

The not unprecedented illogicality of employing violence to end violence (in this novel an armed revolt by German women puts an end to the war) is partially alleviated by Atherton's refusal to give more than a cursory description of the actual combat. This allows her to continue to identify men with the war and women with civilization, as she does in her nonfiction writing:

> The ablest of the male inheritors of the accumulated wisdom and experiences and civilizing influences of the ages were in power prior to August 1914, and not one of them nor all combined had the foresight to circumvent, or the diplomatic ingenuity to keep in leash the panting Hun. They are settling their scores, A.D. 1914–1917, by brute fighting. . . .
> Thinking women . . . may emerge from this hideous reversion of Europe to barbarism with an utter contempt for man. They may despise the men of affairs for muddling Europe into the most terrible war in history. . . . They may experience a secret but profound revulsion from the men wallowing in blood and filth for months on end, living only to kill.[87]

═══ Changing Relationships ═══

The contrast between the experiences of men and women during the war and their effect on sexual relations after the war deserves further examination: "some women's writings celebrated a euphoric group experience of a middle class Herland *protected from the battlefront,* capping the prewar rise of the New Woman" (emphasis added).[88] This protection was perceived to be a potent cause of subsequent social and interpersonal discontent. Men in the trenches, so it is argued, engaged in the male work of combat, understandably came to resent what they imagined to be the soft lives women had led. This belief would bear fruit in later literary history: "In postwar literature, many male characters would prefer the companionship of men to that of women whose affections they found trite and sentimental."[89]

Another element in this seedbed of future antagonism between the sexes has been argued to be an ironic perception on men's part that their experience of combat was one of restriction and immobility; for four years, increasingly alienated from the prewar selves who had experienced independence as their birthright, they had been immobile, trapped in trenches, while the young women of England appeared to have been at liberty in farm and factory, becoming ever more powerful. "Jean, now, might stand for an avenging fury, one of the Erinnyes who blew the savage claims of conscience in the ears of a world desiring only to be comfortable; she would make a good war poster . . . but as the cover for a love story, no, for that she was entirely out of scale."[90]

In the 1914–18 war there was one experience to which women were anterior and that was now claimed by men. What had been predominantly "a disease of women before the war—neurasthenia—became a disease of men in combat . . . physicians immediately recognized the kinship."[91] The contemporary understanding was that neurasthenia was a generalized anxiety syndrome, arising in part from enforced inaction. Showalter identifies the complexity of this sociopsychological dysfunction as exacerbating the perceived rift between the sexes:

> Not surprisingly, hostility towards "beastly" women who were allowed to scream or cry, and whose hysteria had been an accepted form of feminine expression before the war, became the theme of much war literature. Men's quarrels with the feminine element in their own psyches became externalized as quarrels with women, and hysteria expressed itself in part as fear or anger towards the neurotic woman, an anger we see in the war poetry of Owen and Sassoon, in the novels of Aldington and Ford, and in texts such as T. S. Eliot's prose-poem "Hysteria" (1917), where male anxiety is projected onto the devouring female.[92]

Edith Wharton recognized the same conflict in the emotions of the hero of *The Marne*, who is too young to enlist: "France, his France, attacked, invaded, outraged—and he, a poor helpless American boy, who adored her, and could do nothing for her—not even cry, as a girl might! It was bitter."[93]

What elements have we identified as contributing to the hidden subject, the altered perception of sexual identity? On the woman's side there was perceived to be the loss of the old "sweetnesses," the growth of "executive abilities," a questioning of domestic duties, the enjoyment of the independence that war brought, the assumption of men's jobs and roles. On the other side, it was argued that resentment of women's safety and the frustration of "enforced inaction" had alienated men. Although for the duration it was feared that the war would alienate the sexes, this belief became culturally embedded only *after* the war. It is important to emphasize that what has been offered as a general picture of mutual antagonism is found, on closer inspection, to be limited to a few writers, to be more important as a partial representation of a more significant subject (the reconceptualization of gender roles), and, moreover, to be more a postwar construct than a contemporary truth.[94] As Claire Tylee notes: "it was the *construction* of the reality of the War that came between men and women" (emphasis added).[95] James Longenbach persuasively presents this position when he argues that the

> distortion of the war's effect on sexual politics is itself historically important; while it is clear that the Great War was not the point of origin for the rising tensions between men and women (any more than it was the origin of the modernist revolution in the arts), it quickly became *perceived* as such because people who lived through these troubled years (as well as the historians and literary critics who have documented them) were soothed by the idea that social tensions had a point of origin that was fixed and thrust upon them by powers divorced from personal experience.[96]

The gloomy predictions about future sexual relationships inevitably compounded already complex and profound feelings. To the guilt of the survivor was added an often-expressed fear that between the sexes there would grow up what Vera Brittain variously called ". . . a barrier of indescribable experience. . . . a permanent impediment to understanding. . . . that terrible barrier of knowledge. . . . the inevitable barrier—the almost physical barrier of horror and dreadful experience . . . war's dividing influence. . . ."[97] Storm Jameson, five years after the war had ended, wrote that the "gulf which divides the women of my generation and their men who fought in the War is impassable on any terms."[98] Richard Aldington's George Winterbourne talks of "the widening gulf which was separating the men of that generation from the women." The metaphor he uses to illustrate the point brings us almost full circle by reflecting another variant on combat as the only criterion for war literature: "The friends of a person with cancer haven't got cancer . . . aren't in *the horrid category of the doomed.*"[99] The "category of the doomed" was perceived to exclude women, and its use was part of the encoding of "war's dividing influence" into contemporary culture.

Mildred Aldrich is making only a modest query when she asks: "I often wonder if some of the women are not better off than in the days before the war. They do about the same work, only they are not bothered by their men . . . for nearly two years they have had no drinking man to come home at midnight either quarrelsome or sulky. . . . They have lived in absolute peace. . . . I am afraid the next generation is going to be different and the disturbing thing is that it is the women who are changing."[100] The imbalance between what she asks and how she asks it is revealing. Note how often she expresses concern ("wonder . . . afraid . . . disturbing"); how thoughts can be expressed only in the negative ("are not better off . . . are not bothered . . . had no drinking man"). She can begin to consider a future disjunction between the sexes, but cannot allow herself to consider whence it might have come. She puts her inquiry at one remove from herself by establishing it as a problem for the next generation, not herself.

Most women were not antagonistic to men; feelings of loss, bereavement, pity, and guilt were much more common responses. For them the contrast between their wartime experience and the death and mutilation of so many men was experienced as guilt—Sinclair's "shame of . . . immunity." There was even a half-conscious fear that they might in some inexplicable way be the perpetrators of an unspeakable crime. "Because wives, mothers, and sweethearts were safe on the home front, did the war appear in some peculiar sense their fault, a ritual sacrifice to their victorious femininity?"[101] We may object to the phrase "victorious femininity," but Gilbert is posing a perceptive question.

In *The Return of the Soldier,* Rebecca West recounts the story of Capt. Chris Baldry. When he goes to war, Jenny, his cousin and his wife's companion, feels confident that "he loved the life he had lived with us and desired to carry with him to the dreary place of death and dirt the completest picture of everything about his home, on which his mind could brush when things were at their worst, as a man might finger an amulet through his shirt."[102] This belief is shattered when, after a year at the front, Chris tries to deal with his war experiences through shell shock and amnesia, and on his return to the elegant home and wife that he cannot remember, reverts to his first love, a care-worn, working-class woman. In the time before his recovery, Jenny comes to realize that the home and the life she and Kitty, his wife, had created were not in fact what Chris had wanted and had been for their own advantage. It is not too much of an analytical leap to see that although he has been fighting for the England that the house and the women represent, the realities of the front have brought him to the realization that they mean nothing to him.

And there is more. George Parfitt tells only half of the story when he says that "West's novel suggests that the kind of England [they represent] . . . has responsibility for the war and, having allowed war, can only destroy its own."[103] The kind of England that destroys its own has clearly been constructed by women. Their collusion is revealed, but it is only Chris who must go back to the front, "to that flooded trench in Flanders under that sky more full of flying death than clouds, to that No Man's Land where bullets fly like rain on the rotting faces of the dead."[104]

West concentrated more on an analysis of women's sense of guilt than on men's repugnance. In *Mrs. Dalloway,* Virginia Woolf directs most of her commentary on the war onto the figure of the shell-shocked veteran Septimus Warren Smith, but not all of it. Mrs. Dalloway herself thinks that the "War was over, except for someone like Mrs. Foxcroft at the Embassy last night eating her heart out because that nice boy was killed and now the old Manor House must go to a cousin; or Lady Bexborough who opened a bazaar, they said, with the telegram in her hand, John, her favourite, killed; but it was over; thank Heaven—over."[105]

And even Peter Walsh, not the most sensitive of men, is not immune to its influence. In the section of the novel that includes the mysterious gray nurse, Woolf provides a complex insight into how it has affected his perceptions of women. On the way to Regent's Park he has been thinking of his own historical position, "from a respectable Anglo-Indian family which for at least three generations had administered the affairs of a continent (it's strange, he thought, what a sentiment I have about that, disliking India, and empire, and army as he did)," yet he still feels "moments of pride in England." Sitting down beside the elderly gray nurse, who is knitting and who seems "like the champion of the rights of sleepers," he falls asleep. There follows a mysterious two-page dream in which the nurse is one of the central characters, a "giant figure at the end of the ride"; the other is Walsh himself, who appears as a "solitary traveller." The giant figure soon becomes one with the leaves and branches, and all the attributes of womanhood are hers: she is majestic, dispensing "charity, comprehension, absolution," yet capable of "wild carouse." Even when the ever-fluctuating image of green leaves takes a liquid form ("green sea waves . . . rise to the surface . . . fishermen . . . floods . . . float . . . troubled sea") still there showers "down from her magnificent hands, compassion, comprehension, absolution." But the figure is also a siren; a vision, "often overpowering the solitary traveller and taking away from him the sense of the earth," who might blow him "to nothingness with the rest."[106] The traveler continues to move toward her, and soon he is

> beyond the wood; and there, coming to the door with shaded eyes, possibly to look for his return, with hands raised, with white apron blowing, is an elderly woman who seems (so powerful is this infirmity) to seek, over the desert, a lost son; to search for a rider destroyed; to be the figure of the mother whose sons have been killed in the battles of the world. So, as the solitary traveller advances down the village street where the women stand knitting and the men dig in the garden, the evening seems ominous; the figures still; as if some august fate, known to them, awaited without fear, were about to sweep them into complete annihilation.[107]

Walsh wakes up "with extreme suddenness, saying to himself 'The death of the soul,' " and the phrase stays with him.[108]

How should we read this passage? The book's concern with the war, the immediate patriotic context of the dream, as well as internal references, suggest that the war is a significant element of the dream. In which case, what is the role of the nurse? She is protective, she offers solace and understanding as well as protection[109]; but she is also threatening. At the dream's conclusion, the traveler and the women appear together in a range of war-related references: "shaded eyes, possibly to look for his return . . . a lost son . . . destroyed . . . the mother whose sons have been killed in the battles of the world." Here she is the bereaved—but notice the sense of complicity in the final sentence: "So, as the solitary traveller advances down the village street where the women stand knitting and the men dig in the garden, the evening seems ominous; the figures still; as if some august fate, known to them, awaited without fear, were about to sweep them into complete annihilation." The nurse, the bereaved mother, the knitting women, have all led up to the final ominous tableau. Gilbert suggests that "Woolf's grey nurse . . . threatens simultaneously to anoint and annihilate."[110] But what Woolf has brought together are four images of women that she implies were held by men after the war: they offer care, they are powerful, they are bereaved, they are complicit in the war.

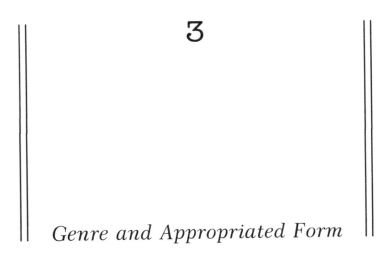

3

Genre and Appropriated Form

> Only the history of . . . forms themselves can provide an adequate mediation between the perpetual change of social life on the one hand, and the closure of the individual work on the other.
>
> —Frederic Jameson

THE LITERATURE OF WORLD WAR I MIGHT NOT APPEAR TO OFFER fertile ground for a study of genre. Indeed, much testimony exists of the way that the sudden shock of immersion in trench warfare was an experience that defied the capacity of existing literary conventions.[1] Those who experienced combat found it extremely difficult to represent what had happened; for some, it was literally indescribable. The effort to record it involved finding a new language and a new style—a process which, in Paul Fussell's words in *The Great War and Modern Memory*, involved "leaving, finally, the nineteenth century behind."[2] These words also suggest the degree to which war writing has now become absorbed into the history of modernism and the way it tends to share that movement's modes of writing and its general emphasis on a break with the past. This fracture became more perceptible as the war receded: in 1940 Virginia Woolf could look back and see World War I as "a chasm in a smooth road"[3]; at the time, however, as much of her writing from the war years testifies, she perceived the process as neither simple nor sudden.

The Great War and Modern Memory takes as its subject precisely the meeting place between Frederic Jameson's "change of social life" and the history of the forms in which that change was represented. It explores the process by which the war was assimilated into metaphor and myth. In particular, in a chapter titled "Myth, Ritual and Romance," Fussell traces the different ways in which the experience of the trenches was perceived as belonging to a different world—a world full of "secrets, conversions, metamorphoses, and rebirths . . . a world of reinvigorated myth."[4] For many soldiers the war experience resembled a medieval quest, he writes, a quest whose shape was defined by the routine of the journey to the front and the rituals of "going up the line,"[5] but also a quest in the sense that such experience was rendered intelligible only through such routine and convention. To express the new meanings and experiences the war created, writers looked for "precedent motifs and images": these came typically from redactions of romance in the nineteenth century—Lord Tennyson's Malory, William Morris's *The Well at the World's End*—as well as from an older source, *The Pilgrim's Progress*. Thus for countless observers, as Fussell notes, " 'the Slough of Despond' was invoked as the only adequate designation for churned-up mud morasses pummelled by icy rain and heavy shells: it becomes one of the inevitable clichés of memory."[6]

Such a revival of romance in war writing may at first appear to be a simple anachronism: the resuscitation of a genre that, having already undergone many transformations since its origin, could now lay claim to no more than a very narrow, fundamentally patriotic ideology. This may be the case with the war adventure story, which appealed to "a generation to whom terms like heroism or decency and nobility . . . were entirely secure," as Fussell notes, and which had an afterlife, described in Orwell's essay "Boys' Weeklies," that extended to World War II.[7]

But by the beginning of the twentieth century, romance had become a very broad category, recognized more as a literary quality than a fixed form. As Gillian Beer writes in *The Romance*, this quality might present itself as "day-dream, allegory, history, fairy-tale, horror-tale, psychological fantasy. All could be claimed as romances."[8] More important was the traffic that romance permitted between these imaginative modes and those—predominantly the realistic novel—which represented and interpreted the known world. It is possible to trace this mix—which had become familiar perhaps by the early twentieth century—in many of the hybrid war narratives mingling actuality with fantasy: the experience of nursing, for example, with the wish fulfillment of a romance plot.[9]

The romance was also able to give shape to a variety of quite disparate experiences of the war. Much of Fussell's work demonstrates the ways in which the principal conventions of romance—the hazardous journey, the nightmare landscape, "ordeal" in its various manifestations, the confrontation of opposing values—responded to the actuality of war. But romance was also capable of expressing the emotional and psychological reverberations of the war for those who watched from the margins—May Sinclair's "fever of longing for danger,"[10] which she felt when serving as a nurse in Belgium. But above all, romance was a form that responded to the *social* conditions of the war. As Frederic Jameson explains it, the romance could express "a transitional moment, yet one of a very special type: its contemporaries must feel their society torn between past and future in such a way that the alternatives are grasped as hostile but somehow unrelated worlds."[11] The pressure of the war was not merely military: it created great social tensions and social choices that were felt in different ways by different groups. Romance provided a literary mode that could express the experience of soldiers in an unprecedentedly ferocious combat, but for other groups, particularly women, it offered different, yet equally valuable, possibilities.

In women's writing the conjunction of mode and moment is especially interesting. For them the war offered extraordinary, if temporary, social opportunities that created in their writing a vivid sense of a society "torn between past and future" as women worked in factories, served overseas, and achieved a kind of independence hitherto unfamiliar. But women were aware of the incongruity between their old and new lives and of the potential conflict between them: some of those who wrote during and immediately after the war (1915–20) attempted to respond to these convergent pressures. This emerges, in the first instance, not through the development of completely new modes of writing but through the adaptation and "mix" of existing genres. This is particularly true of the way women appropriated the genre of romance.

Although it is correct to speak of the "revival" of romance precipitated by the war, the mode and its variations already existed in women's writing. Indeed, it has been argued that women writers were particularly accustomed to translating their experiences into mixed modes: feminist studies such as Sandra Gilbert and Susan Gubar's *The Madwoman in the Attic* maintain, for example, that nineteenth-century women writers were adept at containing romance and fantasy under an essentially realistic narrative surface.[12] This approach has in turn been adapted and extended by Rachel Blau DuPlessis in her examination of the versatile solutions that twentieth-century women writers have brought to nineteenth-century narrative problems, specifically the problems of representing women within the romance plot of love and marriage. Her study illuminates the ways in which women tried to enlarge narrative possibilities by "writing beyond the ending" (the study's title), by developing a critique of dominant narrative strategies, and by discovering or proposing new social formations: "reparenting, woman-to-woman and brother-to-sister bonds . . . forms of communal protagonist."[13]

It is well known that the war was a catalyst for such relationships; women not only found new roles but achieved new social groupings as nurses, munitions workers, drivers, and Land Girls. Their place in the war effort and in the rhetoric and the history of the conflict is becoming familiar. One example, from the 1915 volume of the *Times History of the War*, is a photograph entitled "Around the Statue of Joan of Arc: British Military Nurses at Le Havre."[14] It depicts a group of nurses, plump and bonneted, clustering rather incongruously around the figure of Saint Joan in armor. Its message is clear: these nurses have found a heroic role model. But what may be overlooked is the way the image represents a new social formation, one that could be represented in women's writing about the war. Although this type of change might be thought to belong in its customary preserve, social history, it can also find a place in the history of genre, whose concerns are to a large extent social, in terms of both the ways in which new social formations are represented and of the consequent changes in the relationship between writers and readers (producers and public) that such changes imply. The study of genre also offers an alternative focus to the issues of authenticity and authorship examined in chapter 2; it raises questions of whether women's writing engaged with new social groupings in a deliberate or sustained way; and it raises the further question of the ways in which women, through the adaptation and modification of genres, attempted to find new roles *as writers*.

It is striking to see the speed and self-consciousness with which women sought to record their own experience and the way they looked for forms that would enable them to do this. For women, as much as men, the war was "a literary war."[15] They worked with energy: May Sinclair spent three weeks in Belgium in September 1914 with a British volunteer ambulance corps; her *Journal of Impressions in Belgium* was published by the middle of 1915; she reworked this material as a novel, *The Romantic*, which was published in 1920. Enid Bagnold served as a driver in France after the armistice. She wrote daily letters to her parents numbered so they would know if one were missing. Back at home her mother typed them out for her daughter to use as background for the novel she was to write later. Cicely Hamilton converted the draft of a suffrage novel into a war novel; Katherine Mansfield reconstructed a sexual escapade into a war story within weeks of the event. All, with the exception of Mansfield, who is discussed later, published their work between 1918 and 1920. Their response to the war is immediate, almost opportunistic in some instances: for these reasons it forms part of the first generation of women's war writing.

The following discussion looks at the way in which these women cast their war experiences as romance and, more specifically, as quests. They wrote within the same general context as men, but their position—even for those serving in France—was different. Their quests seem to be infused with a more immediate awareness of the war as the occasion or catalyst for wider social change; acknowledging this in print seemed almost part of the venture. Although many forecasts were optimistic, they could equally be tinged with the kind of disappointment Katherine Mansfield expressed about the postwar world as it was reflected in Virginia Woolf's *Night and Day*: "There *must* have been a change of heart. It is really fearful to see the 'settling down' of human beings. I feel it in the *profoundest* sense that nothing can ever be the same—that, as artists, we are traitors if we feel otherwise: we have to take it into account and find new expressions, new moulds for our thoughts and feelings. . . . We have to face our war."[16]

These quest stories were not Mansfield's "new mould" in any very permanent sense: although their subject matter was new, their narrative format remained traditional. They did, however, represent an attempt to mediate between more conventional representations of women and "new expressions," and in the process they suggest, with different degrees of literary awareness and sophistication, the social instability of the postwar years. In this context it is worth starting with a story that is in many ways an enigma.

═ The Women's War Romance ═

It would be surprising if the publishers' lists of 1918 were to yield a more backward-looking narrative than Dorothy Stanley's *Miss Pim's Camouflage*. Perdita Pim, unmarried, middle-aged, preoccupied by the affairs of house and garden, discovers that she can become invisible. When she reports this talent to the military authorities they send her on an intelligence mission through occupied France to Germany. This she accomplishes successfully and, having passed through assorted perils, returns in possession of information that will save the Allied cause.

In its surface detail Miss Pim's story seems consciously anachronistic. It traverses a landscape whose nature partakes of different elements of romance. It can be chivalric: " 'here is the only old tree of the Bois des Chevaliers, the Chene du Couvent.' Miss Pim looked up at the oak mighty in girth but rather dwarfed in stature. The old twisted branches were rather poor in leafage, but for all that it was noble, and it represented to Miss Pim's imagination the British Oak."[17] The landscape of the cities of Germany is represented as infernal: "people walking listlessly in mourning, anxious and downcast . . . the melancholy pallor of the faces . . . all prowling about with the same obsession—the hunt for food." And it becomes purgatorial, as when she recrosses the field of fire and loses, in the process, "all sense of personal existence; . . . it seemed to Miss Pim that she was wandering in chaos, there was no indication of British lines, no goal to make for, nothing but mud and destroyed things; there was no longer any meaning to anything, the shameful treatment of all things from a strand of barbed wire to human lives, took possession of her mind."[18]

The configurations of a journey to the underworld and back suggest the way that the novel's topography serves as a metaphor for the patriotic cause. This is reinforced by a narrative characterized by a series of episodic adventures and by the extreme simplicity of characterization (where the name Perdita itself announces the romance connection). Miss Pim's quest offers no room for intellectual doubt or moral struggle; indeed, like the protagonist of medieval romance, her function is more that of an observer, the spectator of conflict: "surely this was the Evil One who had to be loosed a little season out of his prison, and who went out to deceive nations which are in the four quarters of the earth, to gather them together to battle, the number of whom is as the sand of the sea."[19]

The novel's ferocious patriotism, which here depicts the Kaiser as an almost magical "opposite,"[20] the scion of a perverted order, suggests a kinship between *Miss Pim's Camouflage* and John Buchan's chauvinistic adventure stories, which were written throughout the war years and featured the patriotic exploits of Richard Hannay. The novel reveals similar links with the war fantasies that Orwell saw as part of the stock in trade of the popular fiction: "conservative . . . in a completely 1914 style," class-bound, unswervingly patriotic, tending to characterize foreigners as sinister or comic or both.[21]

But it is clear that its first readers may not have found the peculiar mix of *Miss Pim's Camouflage* so readily intelligible. Commenting on its blend of contemporary subject matter and archaic patriotism—"about" the war yet almost entirely untainted by contact with its reality—the reviewer in the *Times Literary Supplement* commented, "she does not seem always to have made up her mind what story she has to tell." For this 1918 reader *Miss Pim's Camouflage* was an "extravaganza," a story of wish fulfillment—such "fancies as might come . . . to any old spinster who chafed at her own uselessness."[22]

But this strange coupling of patriotic fantasy with exploration of women's wartime roles is not developed; there is no critique of women's roles, no attempt at social analysis. Instead, these issues remain submerged. The treatment of gender is ambiguous: the narrative announces at the outset that the heroine "should have been the boy" in the family, the boy who "would have become another General Pim and gained a V.C." The tendency toward the male is reinforced by the fact that the successful pursuit of her quest depends not only on the suppression of visibility but also, by implication, on the suppression of femininity: her "camouflage" can be penetrated by children who see through to the woman beneath. But the narrative maintains a realistic surface, which means that these ideas are expressed with a degree of uneasiness. Miss Pim's survival depends on her extraordinary gift: "a curious crick in the neck—like a slight dislocation . . . absence of body! That was just it, the most blood-freezing experience anyone could have. She might have thought it a delusion." While the apparent necessity to render this gift "natural" as an attribute of middle age, suitable for a protagonist who is unmarried and "a rather stout woman of fifty" is almost comic, it is also part of the general evasion of the problems of woman's role and position.[23]

It is appropriate to see such omissions and suppressions as part of the narrative's overall conservatism. But their presence, half visible, suggests the story might be understood as a quest in more ways than one. Alongside the search for military secrets lies the scarcely articulated quest for woman's role in the war. As such, *Miss Pim's Camouflage* becomes a piece of narrative wish fulfillment: it approaches the description of romance given by Northrop Frye as the "search of the libido or the desiring self for fulfilment that will deliver it from the anxieties of reality but will still contain that reality."[24] Nevertheless, at its end—in which the heroine modestly returns to England, home, and garden—the narrative reaches not so much fulfillment as familiar compromise. It becomes an adventure that is not so much resolved as shut down: " 'Everyone says you were wonderful,' remarked Lesley . . . 'But' she continued, 'as I said to George, no one who *really* knew you, could believe you would do anything wonderful. Now, if only George had been sent, what might he not have achieved!'"[25]

For the modern reader, *Miss Pim's Camouflage* is a story that has not "come out." It hints at a struggle against the restrictions on women's adventures, against the narrowness of their roles, and suggests a degree of unease with the way these were traditionally represented. But the novel's failure to engage openly with these issues means that its significance is also limited, especially as an account of women's writing in the war. The traditional adventure story is interesting only in what it reveals about the potentialities for the quest story, not for any fully realized achievement of its own. Thus the discussion that follows lays aside questions of the value of *Miss Pim's Camouflage* and looks at the varied ways that romance and quest were able to express the experience of war.

Despite its ambiguities, Miss Pim's adventure follows a fundamentally patriotic script. By contrast, Cicely Hamilton's *William—An Englishman* uses romance as a means to explore and question established beliefs. Her narrative is a two-stage quest, which as it unfolds reveals the poverty of some prewar idealisms. Its first, perhaps more striking, stage recounts the experiences of a young English couple (they are socialist, pacifist, suffragist) whose wedding journey in the Ardennes is cut short by the German invasion of Belgium. Hamilton represents their sequestered idyll, their absorption in their own kind of politics, their insulation from the events overtaking them through a mixture of comedy and foreboding:

> [William] held up a finger, and Griselda asked "What is it?"
>   "Guns," he said. "Cannon—don't you hear them?"
>   She did; a soft, not unpleasing thud, repeated again and again, and coming down the breeze from the northward.

"It must be manoeuvres," he explained. "That's what those soldiers are doing. I expect it's what they call the autumn manoeuvres."
"Playing at murder," Griselda commented, producing the ortho-
dox sigh. She had heard the phrase used by a pacifist orator in the
Park and considered it apt and telling. "What a waste of time—and
what a brutalising influence on the soldiers themselves! Ah, if only
women had a say in national affairs!"[26]

A series of ordeals follows: in the course of their attempts to evade the
Germans and return to England they are attacked and imprisoned; they
witness the execution of civilians; they are subjected to forced labor, to rape,
and to bombardment. These events are dramatically and powerfully narrated
as is the couple's flight from the Ardennes (described as "Arden"), which is
represented as a heavily charged mythological journey, a perilous escape that
marks the abandonment of their pacifism: "Once [William] found himself
sitting with Griselda under a beech-tree, holding her fingers and considering
how they had come there and why they had got to go on; and wandering off
into vague recollection of the story of a knightly lover who had carried his
mistress long miles through forest in his arms. The details of the story escaped
his memory, and he sought them with a pettish insistence."[27]

But the story is not simply a magical journey toward enlightenment.
The war is destructive; the narrative, through the simple sequence of events,
accomplishes the dismemberment of their former beliefs and the destruction
of the political basis of their relationship. Griselda (the name suggests her
role) dies, incoherently rehearsing old political martyrdoms, and William
escapes as a refugee and eventually returns to England a changed man. The
process of disenchantment is completed, for William, in a second, consider-
ably grimmer stage of the novel in which he is "converted to militarism" and
joins the army, but is not strong enough for combat.[28] He dies in an air raid
while serving as a clerk in France.

In this sequence the romance begins to modulate. There are passages
in which William's former desires and ideals surface intermittently: he "visu-
alised himself as a soldier—an unscientific combatant of the Homeric pattern,
but nevertheless a soldier." He feels, occasionally, the potency of his patriotism: "the fierce flashes in the evening sky were war, real war made visible
and wickedly beautiful; such war as he had seen in the Ardennes village,
and such as he had dreamed of fighting when he first donned his khaki
tunic." But while his vision of war remains romantic and almost archaic, as
the language suggests (and which is discussed further in chapter 4), the
final sequences of the novel reveal the war as a modern industrialized combat,
an affair of routine, almost. William finally realizes his unimportance in "the
machine" in which he dies: "His death, duly entered in the hospital books,
was reported to the Casualty Department and the Graves Registration clerks
took note of his burial and filed it for possible inquiries."[29]

A quest so completely frustrated turns toward tragedy: "all the more pitiful because he is commonplace," one reviewer noted. "Real tragedy chooses the most unlikely actors."[30] This generic shift is arguably central to the novel: it blurs the simple oppositions of the first phase—the romantic idyll contrasted with the portrayal of German brutality, for example. As William's comprehension of the war deepens, he comes to reject old formulas and realizes "the impossibility of fitting all men to one pattern and of solving the problems of human misgovernment and government by means of the simple and sweeping expedients he had once been so glib in upholding."[31]

Hamilton uses the generic shift as a way of representing the change of consciousness; published in 1919, the novel is concerned with the early phases of the war and with the growth and change in awareness of what it signified. This is the essence of what Nicola Beauman calls the novel's "immediacy."[32] The significance of the novel's shifting strata has often escaped the attention of modern commentators, who have labeled it as merely patriotic—"somewhat of an after-the-fact propaganda piece"—or outdated—"of a piece with the propaganda writing from early on in the First World War."[33]

The protagonist's realization of the nature of the war was paralleled, perhaps, by Hamilton's own. Her autobiographical memoir, *Life Errant*, which appeared in 1935, indicates that *William—An Englishman* was only "accidentally" a war novel:

> It was really a suffrage novel; its outline had taken shape in my thoughts before there was any suspicion of the war to come and its beginnings I date from a gathering where I heard certain members of the militant section hold forth on the subject of their "war." Most politicians indulge in exaggerated speech and the suffragette was no exception to the rule; on this particular occasion "deputations" to Parliament and encounters with the Police were described in terms of stricken fields. I found myself wondering, as I listened to the speeches, what the "warriors" would feel if they were pitchforked into the real thing—and the idea amused and attracted me. I had no more understanding than the average civilian of what warfare under modern conditions would mean; but I did understand that it meant something more dangerous . . . than rough-and-tumbles round the House of Commons; and that being the case, I decided that here was material for a story; a young man and woman, enthusiastic, ignorant, who had thought of their little political scuffles as a war and who stumbled accidentally into the other kind of war—of bullets and blood and high explosives.[34]

Hamilton's testimony confirms what one might call the novel's revisionism: the changing attitude to the war that is signaled by the accompanying shift in genre. The comments above suggest that her personal revision continued well into the 1930s, but the novel's date of publication, 1919, suggests that it reflects directly the general mix of feelings at the war's end through its preoccupation with changing perceptions of the war and with the ways that simple idealisms were overcome by the realities of the conflict. *William— An Englishman* belongs to the immediate postwar period almost by virtue of these mixed attitudes and modes: it works through broad-brush contrasts and explores the war's impact on an ordinary and naïve protagonist. Its immediacy is produced by the contrast and shift of feeling and by the growth of new but inchoate perceptions; to judge it merely in terms of its dominant elements as do Philip Hager and Claire Tylee, is to mistake both form and context.

Where Hamilton's story works by modifying the format of romance as war adventure, May Sinclair's *The Romantic*, published in 1920, seems to offer a different kind of immediacy: her novel, based closely on her brief war service in Belgium, explores the issue of cowardice in combat, and it does so from a woman's point of view. In these ways, and in contrast to the works discussed so far, Sinclair's novel promises a narrative whose main focus is on issues of gender.

The Romantic attempts to combine both types of romance narrative, the quest for love and the quest for truth. Charlotte Redhead, serving with an ambulance corps in Belgium, discovers that John Conway, the man she loves, is a coward: he abandons his wounded and escapes into safety; several times he deserts dying men in a crisis. The heroine thus becomes divided between her desire to serve honorably in the war and her desire to remain with Conway. Her pursuit of the truth about her companion finally forces her to confront the fact of his fear and to accept its consequences, which involve both the destruction of the relationship and the death of Conway.

In several ways Sinclair's story uses the war as a pretext. Conway hopes that sharing the adventure of serving in Belgium with Charlotte will serve as a substitute for his sexual failure: " 'Unless you can go into it as if it was some tremendous, happy adventure—that's the only way to take it. I shouldn't be any good if I didn't feel it was the most *romantic* thing that ever happened to me.' " This is a strategy that inevitably involves some elaborate idealizations and deceptions—" 'you're like Jeanne d'Arc [he declares] . . . in a helmet, looking down, with big, dropped eyelids' "—but ends, equally inevitably, in a series of failures, with sexual failure represented through the failure belonging predominantly to war, cowardice.[35] The narrative is a kind of case history: it is preoccupied with the individual instance. But it is also constructed around the events and setting of the British withdrawal from Belgium and suggests, in Claire Tylee's words, the "equation of the dejectedness of a retreating army with the anticlimax of sexual failure."[36]

The Romantic also uses the war as a pretext in a more literal and fundamental sense, as an event that offered new experiences to women and that provided the conditions, physical and emotional, for roles to be reversed. This is signaled by the highly confident narrative voice:

> It was an hour since they had left Newhaven.
> The boat went steadily, inflexibly, without agitation, cutting the small crisp waves with a sound like the flowing of stiff silk. For a moment after the excited rushing and hooting, there had been something not quite real about this motion, till suddenly you caught the rhythm, the immense throb and tremor of the engines.
> Then she knew.
> She was going out, with John and Gwinnie Denning and a man called Sutton, Dr. Sutton, to Belgium, to the war. She wondered whether any of them really knew what it would be like when they got there.[37]

This confidence is developed through Charlotte's growing independence and self-awareness during her time in Belgium: "going by herself was better than going with a man who funked it."[38] It is also supported by the way Sinclair appropriates incidents from the war to represent episodes in the developing psychological drama. A particularly striking example of this is Conway's attempt to make her see bravery as futile by showing her the corpses stacked in a makeshift mortuary: " 'Look there—' he said. The dead men were laid out in a row, on their backs; grayish white, sallow-white faces upturned; bodies straight and stiff on a thin litter of straw. Pale gray light hovered, filtered through dust. It came from some clearer place of glass beyond that might have been a carpenter's shop, partitioned off. She couldn't see what was going on there. She didn't see anything but the dead bodies, the dead faces, and John's living face."[39] The growing preoccupation with interior drama tends to diminish the role of the narrative: the resolution (in which the coward dies) is less important than the process of psychological stripping away of the layers of truth; the slow movement toward recognition takes precedence over the external events of the war, which eventually serve merely as props and stage effects.

The narrative half-acknowledges the problems that follow from Charlotte's using the war as part of what is fundamentally a strategy of displacement: " 'All that war-romancing. I see how awful it was. When I think how we went out and got thrills. Fancy getting thrills out of this horror.' "[40] This kind of compunction limits the narrative's ability to raise speculative issues; the novel also limits and internalizes such questioning by having a narrow ideological scope, a traditional narrative structure, and a reluctance to develop related issues, such as that of female sexuality:

> He stood close, close in front of her, tall and strong and handsome in his tunic, knee breeches, and puttees. She could feel the vibration

of his intense, ardent life, of his excitement. And suddenly, before his young manhood, she had it again, the old feeling, shooting up and running over her, swamping her brain. She wondered with a sort of terror whether he would see it in her face, whether if she spoke he would hear it thickening her throat. He would loathe her if he knew. She would loathe herself if she thought she was going into the war because of that, because of him.[41]

The Romantic has the potential to be a story of feminine liberation. But Sinclair concludes her narrative ambiguously. It appears to achieve a degree of finality and resolution in the death of Conway; in the return of the ambulance corps to England; in the suggestion, no more, that Charlotte may find happiness with another. But the very number of these alternatives suggests that resolving the problem of Conway is an awkward affair. The narrative closure is reinforced, rather uneasily, by a final conversation in which Sinclair tries to bring home her diagnosis: "[H]e couldn't live a man's life. He was afraid to enter a profession. He was afraid of women. . . . All that romancing was a gorgeous transformation of his funk. . . . In a sense the real John Conway was the man who dreamed."[42]

Although *The Romantic* demonstrates the way that the romance might be adapted and reshaped as a speculative, internalized quest, it achieves this only by exhibiting a kind of single-mindedness that involves excluding many of the issues surrounding the problem of cowardice: the strains of traditional gender roles, for men as well as women; the social values—weakness, cowardice, masculinity—that underlie these ideas. Despite its potential as a feminist text, a possible exemplar of Sandra Gilbert's argument that the war allowed repressed social and psychological aspirations to run free,[43] *The Romantic* remains a war adventure, cautious both in the conclusions it draws and the approach to genre it displays. It was left to other women writers to attempt to reshape this mold.

In some ways Enid Bagnold's *The Happy Foreigner*, published in 1920, offers a parallel to Sinclair's *The Romantic*: it combines material taken from her own experience as an ambulance driver in France with a romance plot. Bagnold's heroine, Fanny, arrives in France after the armistice to drive for the French army. The routine of driving—rain, mud and sleet, fatigue, sleep—is lifted when she meets a young captain, Julien Chatel, whose gaiety and laughter "transform the dreary pattern" of days and nights on the road. From Metz to Precy to Chantilly their paths cross, a series of snatched moments when Fanny, in her one pair of silk stockings, can forget "the daylight image of herself—the khaki figure, the driver."[44]

Predictably, a publisher's blurb draws attention to some of the more sensational transformations—the ambulance driver turned seductress—of the romance of the postwar period. But unlike Sinclair's story, the narrative is also occupied with the more complex shift that has to occur in France as peace is reestablished. This is conveyed through the contrast between the landscapes left behind by war and the signs of peace returning. The countryside is irretrievably marked: "she drove them back through the waking town and out by the Verdun gates, and soon up on to the steep heights above the town among frozen fields and grasslands white with frost. The big stone tombs of 1870 stuck out of a light ground fog like sails upon a grey sea, and it was not long, at Jeandelize, before the 1914 graves began, small, isolated wooden crosses." In the city of Metz, however, a new life is beginning: "They leant from the ambulance excitedly as the lights of the streets flashed past them, saw windows piled high with pale bricks of butter, bars of chocolate, tins of preserved strawberries and jams. 'Can you see the price on the butter?' "[45]

The return of peace is represented through the continual movement and journeyings in the narrative. In this manner the commonplace of the military romance of the liberated woman driver is turned into something akin to a metaphor for the new order, in which the freedom of the heroine keeps step with the transformation of France. This, probably, was the source of Katherine Mansfield's admiration for the story and its heroine, "a pioneer who sees, feels, thinks, hears and yet is herself full of the sap of life."[46]

But although exhilarated and sometimes exaggerated, *The Happy Foreigner* is more than a simplified parable. It represents the winter and spring of 1918–19, a moment of equipoise between devastation and reconstruction; it observes sharply the postwar mood, the psychology of liberation that yearns for butter, jam, and new dresses: "Around the Spanish Square the first sun-awnings had been put up in the night, awnings red and yellow, flapping in the mountain wind. In the shops under the arches, in the market in the centre of the Square, they were selling anemones. 'But have you any eggs?' 'No eggs this morning.' 'Any butter?' 'None. There has been none these three days.' 'Must I eat anemones? Give me two bunches.' "[47]

The narrative acknowledges its portrayal of a mood that is essentially transitory and will not survive the establishment of permanent peace. This will bring new social roles that cannot be reconciled with the present: "The soldier had been a wanderer like herself, a half-fantastic being. But here beside her in the darkness stood the civilian, the Julien-to-come, the solid man, the builder, plotting to capture the future."[48]

The word "half-fantastic" is also indicative of the way the narrative blends fantasy with the depiction of the postwar landscape: a mixture of modes that limits, inevitably, the novel's potential for social analysis but that allows the consciousness of its heroine to dominate to the end. Without doubt this rather solipsistic narrative voice—which describes its heroine with approval as "invincible, inattentive to the voice of the absent man, a hard, hollow goddess, a flute for the piping of heaven"—reflects the general self-consciousness of Bagnold's writing, but it also raises larger questions of interpretation.[49]

= Feminism and the Postwar Romance =

The novels discussed above are notably diverse, even though they share a stock of motifs and narrative configurations. They are predominantly exploratory in tone; they do not speak with one voice about the conflict that was drawing to a close. They neither share a position that could be simply labeled "feminist" nor wholly support, for example, Sandra Gilbert's thesis that the war created an "overt celebration of the release of female desires."[50] Although they are preoccupied with the freedoms the war granted to women, these novels represent "the release of female desires" within, in each case, a more complex set of meanings: the restoration of peace (Bagnold); the revaluation of ideals (Hamilton); the analysis of cowardice (Sinclair); the enactment of a patriotic cause (Stanley).

The feminism displayed in their writings is also tempered by their reluctance to make predictions or give any sense that women's future roles could be foreseen, still less assured.[51] This evidence emerges through the partial and temporizing conclusions of the narratives. Moreover, writing that does describe the emergence of new social roles often charts no more than the discovery itself—for example, the heroic bleakness of Dorothy Canfield's "La Pharmacienne," which initiates its heroine "into a new and awful and wonderful world along a new and thorny and danger-beset path."[52] But there existed many less optimistic forecasts. Rebecca West's *The Return of the Soldier* reverts to the traditional image of women as the keepers of house, the guardians of property and family, the "brilliantly adequate" arrangers of the gracious life who connive to suppress both "adventures" and those feelings or ideals that do not fit the material realities of this life.[53]

The variety, the ideological range and uncertainties of these stories are reflected in the way they use the genre. Although they all possess the ingredients of romance—love story, combat, withdrawal from society, private ideals, emotional extremity, the ecstatic fulfillment of long-suppressed wishes— only in the politically simple-minded *Miss Pim's Camouflage* is it possible to identify without hesitation the romance's pivotal opposition between good and evil. Indeed, those novels which attempt to combine romance as quest and romance as love story have the greatest difficulty in arriving at a clear sense of whether the "opposition," the threat to happiness and security, comes from the military conflict or from *men*. In Sinclair's novel and, in a different way, in Hamilton's, this issue is not resolved. Bagnold's story evades it by selecting a postwar setting and a heroine who is, above all, independent. Only Katherine Mansfield's "An Indiscreet Journey," discussed later, engages with the question by means of adapting the form.

Nevertheless, the ability of a single genre to accommodate such varied narratives is striking. As suggested above, this may be understood as belonging to the inherent capaciousness of the form itself, but it was also precipitated by the social climate of 1918, in which women's suppositions and fantasies during the war years came up against the realities of the postwar reconstruction, with questions about the place of women in the workforce and with what Arthur Marwick called the "stop-go" progress toward emancipation legislation.[54] Nor does such a sense of social change belong only to the historians of the period: much writing in the postwar years bears witness to it, even if few people expressed it as directly as Virginia Woolf:

> [M]entally the change is marked too. Instead of feeling all day & going home through dark streets that the whole people, willing or not, were concentrated on a single point, one feels now that the whole bunch has burst asunder & flown off with the utmost vigour in different directions. We are once more a nation of individuals. Some people care for football; others for racing; others for dancing; others for—oh, well, they're all running about very gaily, getting out of their uniforms and taking up their private affairs again. Coming home from the Club tonight I thought for a moment that it must still be sunset, owing to the sharp bright lights in Piccadilly Circus. The streets are crowded with people quite at their ease; & the shops blazoning unshaded lights. Yet its depressing too. We have stretched our minds to consider something universal at any rate; we contract them at once to the squabbles of Lloyd George, & a General Election.[55]

The atmosphere that Woolf describes is precisely the "transitional moment . . . [the] society torn between past and future in such a way that the alternatives are grasped as hostile but somehow unrelated worlds" to which romance gives expression.[56] Moreover, the mode lingered throughout the postwar decade, renewing and reviving its formal possibilities to fit changing perceptions of the war.

The renewal—in some cases the transformation—of the genre can be traced across women's writing during the decade after the war. At times this is no more than the replication of the familiar narratives of war service, the stories of nurses and drivers. In other instances the adventure story is reshaped to express the new perspectives the 1920s gave to the war. *War Nurse: The True Story of a Woman Who Lived, Loved, and Suffered on the Western Front* was written anonymously by Rebecca West. Like *William—An Englishman* and *The Romantic*, it sets one aspect of its romance, the story of "living and loving," within the formative experience of the war, in this case nursing in a Paris hospital. Although *War Nurse* is a quest in terms of its pursuit of nursing as a "new life," it is a pursuit that is represented with grim realism. It starts with an unusually graphic description of an attempt to extract shrapnel from a soldier's eye. Such frankness and detail clearly place the narrative in the postwar period; its distance from the conflict is also revealed through its persistent focus on the way the war affected the generation who fought and the ways in which it reversed ideas of progress: "When you look at a hospital, don't think of it as a magic-shop where medical science is taking the pain out of warfare," West writes, "think of it as a place where doctors and nurses are doing their best, but can't do more than mitigate a hideousness of suffering that is not so far off the good old-fashioned hell our grandparents believed in." But the novel is also "romance" in the way it compares the opposed worlds of America and Europe: "I learned about New York in that Paris hospital . . . Oh I learned a lot more about New York than the Social Register ever taught me."[57] West suggests that although France retained its status as the place where young Americans gained sexual experience, during the war they gained it with a crude directness, stripped of its prewar glamour and culture:

> But whatever part of the country they came from, the American boys brought a great deal of sexual hysteria with them because of their strange ideas of French morals. Always America has thought of France as a country of pleasure and leisure and release, and Paris as a magical city where by a common understanding you could go and treat yourself to all those indulgences which you denied yourself at home. Of course it's so in England, too, but they're not so respectable as we are in the States, they haven't got quite such a need for imagining a place where they can go on the loose.[58]

Whereas West suggests the way that the war demystified the cultural relationship between Europe and America, other writers took a different, more radical stance toward romance. Remarque's *All Quiet on the Western Front* (1928)—"least of all an adventure, for death is not an adventure to those who stand face to face with it"[59]—provided the cue for the 1930 "*Not So Quiet . . .*" by Evadne Price (pseudonym Helen Zenna Smith), a woman's war story written as a parallel and as a tribute. That neither book is concerned with heroics is plainly conveyed through the narrative structures that replace the sweep of an adventure story with the immediacy of first-person, present-tense narratives, diary-like in their intimacy and detail. Like *All Quiet*, "*Not So Quiet . . .*" presents the war in all its "dailiness"—wounds, lice, the continual meanness of the conflict: "spew and vomit and sweat . . . I had forgotten these words are not used in the best drawing rooms on Wimbledon Common." Moreover, the novels are structurally similar in the way they construct the worlds of the western front and the home front in opposition to each other: it is this opposition, not the international struggle, that becomes the center of the conflict. "Enemies? Our enemies aren't the Germans. Our enemies are the politicians we pay to keep us out of war and who are too damned inefficient to do their jobs properly."[60]

For Price's heroine, the everywoman Smithy, the ignorant and jingoistic world of home becomes increasingly dreamlike and alien: it is a presence—evoked in passages of fantasy, obsessive imagining, and bitter rhetoric—in service of which the ordeal of war service fulfills nothing: "outwardly I am

Smithy, assistant cook; inwardly I am nothing. I have no feelings that are not physical. I dislike being too hot or too cold. My body is healthy, my mind negative. I have no love or hate for anyone. . . . I am content to drift along in the present. The past has gone; I have no future . . . I want no future."[61]

The entire narrative rejects not merely the idea of heroism but also (as the passage above suggests) the individualism of the romance. *"Not So Quiet . . ."* is light years away from Bagnold's "solitary Odyssey in the Renault car" in 1918[62]; it looks, instead, at the *collective* experience of war—collective in that it depicts the experience of a group of women and in that it crosses class divisions in the process. The emphasis is on shared desires—warmth, cleanliness, food; it takes the expression of these shared values further, as Barbara Hardy points out, by creating a "composite" heroine, "Helen Zenna Smith," and the variants on her name—Helen, Nell, Smithy, Smith—that build up in the narrative. It emphasizes the communal in its use of the present tense and the creation of a slow-motion narrative, bound by routine. It is at once a popular novel and, in Barbara Hardy's words, "an argument against separatisms of all kinds"[63]; but it achieves these qualities by steadily dismantling romance values rather than articulating a new political creed.

Both the great popular novels by Price and Remarque were written more than 10 years after the war, and both sought to disprove the notion that adventure or romance had any place in the conflict. But these were not isolated examples; they reflected a change of public mood. By 1930 it was possible to look back and reassess the writing of the war. Opinion had altered: in the words of one commentator in 1930, "we are waking up, and we are turning to the sincere records of the last affair. We are growing disinclined for romantic nonsense. We have come through the heroic mood, and are not so moved as formerly by helpless sobs and laurel wreaths."[64]

Still, much of the writing discussed earlier in this chapter takes a more reflective approach to the conflict than these words might suggest. The earlier novels share more than a collection of motifs: they share a common mood— a sense of the energy, change, and release brought about by the war. Their authors observed emerging social formations and expressed them through different inflections: some optimistic; some conservative; very few completely feminist; many only patchily or subconsciously aware of gender issues; most cautious—often silent, as the resolutions of the novels suggest—in their vision of women's future social roles.

Although the novels are clearly topical—in the way they shape their quests as a journey to the front or raise questions about the way the war influenced issues of women's role and identity—they gain their form from genre: they were conditioned as much by the forms available as Frederic Jameson's "perpetual change of social life." Although the overall *feel* of these romances, their pursuit of an almost indefinable future, can be attributed to the mood of the immediate postwar years, it can also be explained in terms of the evolution of the genre. Jameson argues that "mood" rather than "event" is the means by which modern romance moves toward meaning, but this is something that is constantly promised rather than achieved: "an object world forever suspended on the point of meaning, forever disposed to receive a revelation, whether of evil or of grace, that never takes place."[65] Although such comment can illuminate the works discussed already, it relates much more closely to Katherine Mansfield's "An Indiscreet Journey," a story in which the search for revelation seems to become the subject matter itself.

Mansfield made her journey to the war zone in 1915. Her relationship with her husband, John Middleton Murry, at an impasse, she traveled to the French town of Gray, which was forbidden to women visitors. There she spent a few days with Corp. Francis Carco. There was a close connection between Mansfield's sexual adventures and her literary ones: she kept a diary of the affair; the "indiscreet journey" to Carco was followed shortly—within a month—by her return to France to write, in Carco's Paris flat. It is likely that Mansfield wrote the story at this time, although it was not published until 1924, a year after her death.

The written journey is constructed as two phases. The first, which re-counts the train journey to Gray, builds up the momentum of the adventure—the triumphs over officials, the meeting with her lover, and a family invented for the occasion. But the emphasis is on the search; on the state of mind that desires "indiscretion"; on the constant presence of a jubilant and elated narrative voice that feverishly and promiscuously piles up impressions—a pail of fish; "a tin wine cup stained a lovely impossible pink"[66]; a black velvet toque topped by a sea gull. It is as if the tableaux of a romance are concentrated into the smaller, sharper dimensions of a still life.

This is followed by an episode that transforms the elation of the journey into a series of enigmatic encounters and deceptive appearances: "what an extraordinary thing. We had been there to lunch and to dinner each day; but now in the dusk and alone I could not find it." A restaurant now seems an "empty place that was really a barn"; its wallpaper gives the appearance of "eating one's dinner at all seasons in the middle of a forest." The surroundings and events—the tick of the clock, the "ghostly clatter of the dishes," the counting of the card players, the weeping of a soldier who has been gassed—receive no explanation. All things seem to conspire to promise a meaning that never arrives: "And years passed. Perhaps the war is long since over—there is no village outside at all—the streets are quiet under the grass. I have an idea this is the sort of thing one will do on the very last day of all—sit in an empty cafe and listen to the clock ticking until—"[67]

At its end, the indiscreet journey yields little: it ends with a drinking party in "a dark smelling scullery, full of pans of greasy water, of salad leaves and meat-bones." But this enigmatic ending is, unlike that of the other works discussed, deliberate: the search for an epiphany is met with an open ending and a refusal. "An Indiscreet Journey" is not, as Claire Tylee points out, a simple adventure (one that charts, for example, the loss of virginity); but on the other hand, neither is it merely a social commentary on the war.[68] The story's detachment, neutrality, and power derive from the way it handles the traffic between the physical world and that of the psyche. It journeys through the former at the same time as it explores the latter; it is "about" both the conditions of the war and the states of mind the war engenders. In this it is both clearly and characteristically modernist while retaining its affiliation to older genres—to the fantastic and to the romance.

Mansfield's story raises one other issue: the question of the extent to which she—or any other of these writers—used genre in a way that is specific to women. There are, as the preceding discussion has shown, no simple answers. "An Indiscreet Journey" is feminist in its awareness of the woman's place in a war zone and acutely aware of its mixture of action, observation, and voyeurism. It is possible to set this story alongside Bagnold's *The Happy Foreigner*, even Sinclair's *The Romantic*, and identify the overlapping ways in which these narratives display a self-conscious awareness of women's position as observers of the war, while recounting their own deeds.[69] But an account of romance allows one to go no further than that: its mix of fantasy and realism provided the opportunity for many kinds of analysis in which consciousness of gender was usually only one element in the pattern. Moreover, it is clear that the genre was equally available to men, whether combatant or noncombatant.[70]

The fact that romance flourished as a mode in the war and in the writing of the war may suggest that it was, contrary to the view of Claire Tylee,[71] something more than an "old model" of writing. Rather, romance allowed these writers to respond to a particular moment, a "moment" characterized in the years immediately after the war by a hesitant but optimistic sense of change. Still, the romances discussed are not particularly sustained explorations of the *social* changes brought about by the war. They are constricted in their timescale; they lack a perspective on the prewar period; as indicated, they offer little vision of the future.

They seem narrow, even lightweight, in comparison with some other war writing that employs the same mode—Siegfried Sassoon's *Memoirs of a Fox-Hunting Man* (1928), for example, in which a prewar sequence of pastoral romance, occupying four-fifths of the book, lays the foundation for the contrasts provided by the experience in the trenches. A similar comparison can be drawn with Helen Thomas's accounts of the idyll of her courtship and early married life with Edward Thomas, *As It Was* and *World without End*, a romance broken by the onset of illness and the eruption of the war. The memoirs of Sassoon and Thomas help place the works discussed in this chapter in context. In much postwar writing romance became an essentially nostalgic mode, used increasingly to evoke the prewar years, what came to be seen as the long Edwardian summer, a world opposed to the war by virtue of its peace, its freedom, and its social stability. In such a context the novels discussed in this chapter form a distinctly minority voice: energetic, opportunist, but with a theme that was essentially unsustainable.

Here also, the constituent elements of genre, "the closure of the individual work" and "the perpetual change of social life," illuminate the configurations of women's writing. Although much of women's writing suggests optimism for the future and a view of gender that was not wholly or simply oppositional, there were some for whom the buoyancy of the war years ended in disillusion, even tragedy. These, like Radclyffe Hall's Miss Ogilvy, looked back to the end of the conflict and were forced to recognize that their usefulness was over. In her 1926 story, "Miss Ogilvy Finds Herself," Hall raises the question of what alternatives existed for such women and how they could complete their lives. At the end of the war Miss Ogilvy says goodbye to her drivers and to the ambulance that has seen her through the war: "Miss Ogilvy's heart gave a sudden, thick, thud to see this undignified, pitiful ending; and she turned and patted the gallant old car as though she were patting a well-beloved horse, as though she would say: 'Yes, I know how it feels—never mind, we'll go down together.' "[72]

But the narrative moves rapidly away from this moment of pessimism and, abandoning social problems and social solutions, turns toward a new adventure, toward romance. Miss Ogilvy's search is for her own sexual identity, the theme Hall was to explore again, in a different mode, in *The Well of Loneliness* (1928). Although it is clear that Miss Ogilvy—cropped hair, in her late 50s and unmarried, relation to the opposite sex "unusual"—cannot find a role in postwar society, the narrative mixes social pessimism with a romantic fantasy, which suggests that for women, the quest and all that it promised could never be abandoned finally: "She found herself standing on the mainland one morning looking at a vague blur of green through the mist, a vague blur of green that rose out of the Channel like a tidal wave suddenly suspended. Miss Ogilvy was filled with a sense of adventure; she had not felt like this since the ending of the war. 'I was right to come here, very right indeed. I'm going to shake off all my troubles.' "[73]

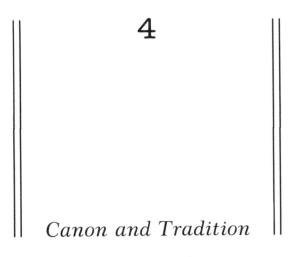

4

Canon and Tradition

On or about December 1910 human nature changed. . . . All human relations shifted—those between masters and servants, husbands and wives, parents and children. And when human relations change there is at the same time a change in religion, conduct, politics and literature.

—Virginia Woolf, "Mr. Bennet and Mrs. Brown"

[I]n this spring and early summer of nineteen-fourteen the old life was over.

—Gertrude Stein, *The Autobiography of Alice B. Toklas*

It was in 1915 the old world ended.

—D. H. Lawrence, *Kangaroo*

IT IS NOT THE FUNCTION OF THIS CHAPTER TO DETERMINE PRE-
cisely when "the old world ended" or how the change affected literature. But

an understanding of the relationship between the Great War, cultural change, and the major literary movements of the early part of the century is a prerequisite to understanding the modern tradition of war writing and how the canon came to be determined.

= Two Vocabularies =

The literary means of dealing with the impact of events of the magnitude of World War I were changing before, during, and after its duration, and the different solutions coexisted. Appeals to traditional perceptions of meaning continued alongside modernist insight, and this duality of vision existed in women writers as well as men. Parfitt sums it up in this way: "novelists who try to say something about the war are led to adopt a variety of angles of vision and types of fictional approach. This variety . . . affects their ways of articulating their visions. Some novelists . . . seem anxious to pretend that old styles and old forms are still adequate for writing about the war, while others are clear that the occasion calls for innovation."[1]

The following excerpt from Mrs. Humphry Ward's novel "*Missing*" employs the old styles and the old forms:

> [the painting] was one of the Turner water-colours which glorified the cottage; the most adorable, she thought, of all of them. It shewed a sea of downs, their grassy backs flowing away wave after wave, down to the real sea in the gleaming distance. Between the downs ran a long valley floor—cottages on it, woods and houses, farms and churches, strung on a silver river; under the mingled cloud and sunshine of an April day. It breathed the very soul of England,—of this sacred long-descended land of ours. Sarratt, who had stood beside her when she had first looked at it, had understood it so at once.
> "Jolly well worth fighting for—this country! isn't it?"[2]

This interpretative description of a rural English scene combines two traditional and related vocabularies—the archaic and the sentimental ("glorified the cottage . . . adorable . . . shewed . . . flowing . . . gleaming . . . silver river . . . mingled cloud and sunshine of an April day . . . the very soul of England . . . this sacred long-descended land"); both are put to pious patriotic use in the thoughts of characters who are at ease with traditional, received ideas.

Such writing coexisted, however, with the following description of a rural French scene from Mary Borden's *The Forbidden Zone*:

> It is the whispering of the grass and the scent of new-mown hay that makes me nervous. . . . the terrible scent of the new-mown hay disturbs me. Crazy peasants came and cut it while the battle was going on just beyond the canal. Women and children came with

pitchforks and tossed it in the sun. Now it lies in the road in the moonlight, wafting its distressing perfume into my window, bringing me . . . unbearable, sickening, intolerable dreams. . . . There has been a harvest. Crops of men were cut down in the fields of France where they were growing. They were mown down with a scythe, were gathered into bundles, tossed about with pitchforks, pitchforked into wagons and transported great distances and flung into ditches and scattered by storms and gathered up again and at last brought here— what was left of them.[3]

Such writing lies athwart that of Ward. It is fantastic, uncomprehending, neurasthenic. The thoughts are those of someone who is insistent on disassociating herself from the unbearable reality that lies behind the scene she is describing. For Borden, though not for Ward, the need to realize a response to the war has of itself rendered a referential style impossible; the war has become what Parfitt calls the occasion of innovation. Nor are these two extremes the only possibilities. Other writers employ neither received sentiment nor the incomprehension of rejection: Beatrice Harraden, for instance, describes the sight of the thousands of tents that made up the Bergen-op-Zoom refugee camp in a detached tone, as a "curious and interesting sight . . . exactly like a scene from a play."[4]

Any radical transformation in experience and perception, however it may be caused, puts considerable stress on writers' sense of appropriate form and style. Some writers, inhibited perhaps by their scruples of what could decently be reported and their belief in the continuity of style, attempted to constrain their writing to what was familiar and to appeal to the sympathy of their readers by invoking traditional pieties—despite the inherent unlikelihood of the familiar being capable of realizing the unprecedented. Others were willing, impelled perhaps, to forge new styles, employ new vocabularies, create new forms. The results of these tensions were numerous, various, and contemporaneous. This chapter will attempt to chart the strategies that women found most appropriate to their writing and to explore the effect their choice of strategy had in terms of the regard in which they came to be held as war writers.

The source material for Vera Brittain's autobiographical memoir, *Testament of Youth*, published in 1933, came from the diary she kept throughout the war, which was itself published in 1982 as *Chronicle of Youth: The War Diary, 1913–1917*. In light of the amount of material contained in the diary and its importance to Brittain, what are we to make of the following extract from *Testament of Youth*? "Perhaps, I thought, Wordsworth or Browning or Shelley would have some consolation to offer; all through the War poetry was the only form of literature that I could read for comfort, and *the only kind that I ever attempted to write*" (emphasis added).[5]

The implicit priority she gives to writing poetry over keeping a diary (although the verse she wrote is now largely forgotten and the diary is still in print) reveals the important position allocated to poetry during the war. We should not read Brittain's comment in the light of our own postwar understanding of war poetry as bitter, cynical, and modernist. She was reflecting the more traditional sense of poetry as the correct form for heroic and inspirational verse. When Mildred Aldrich asks, "Do you ever wonder what the poets of the future will do with this war?"[6] she understands a similar perceived function for poetry as the proper form to record war and its attendant values and emotions.

It is in this sense too that we should understand the following passage from *"Missing,"* in which the same characters who earlier in this chapter had discussed Turner now consider the growing significance of poetry in wartime: " 'Isn't it strange'— her tone was thoughtful—'how people care for poetry nowadays! A few years ago, one never heard of people—ordinary people—*buying* poetry, new poetry—or reading it. But I know a shop in Manchester that's just full of poetry—new books and old books—and the shopman told me that people buy it almost more than anything. Isn't it funny? What makes them do it? Is it the war?' "[7]

Sarratt again fulfills the role of articulating the heroine's inarticulate sentiments and pointing to the moral. His answer also provides a timely warning of the danger for the postwar critic of privileging the cynical above the sentimental as a vehicle for truth. For some writers, the truth can be best captured in the sentimental:

> "I suppose it's the war," he said at last. "It does change fellows. It's easy enough to go along bluffing and fooling in ordinary times. Most men don't know what they think—or what they feel—or whether they feel anything. But somehow—out there—when you see the things other fellows are doing—when you know the things you may have to do yourself . . . it doesn't seem unnatural—or hypocritical— or canting—to talk and feel—sometimes—as you couldn't talk or feel at home, with life going on just as usual. I've had to censor letters, you see, darling—and the letters some of the roughest and stupidest fellows write, you'd never believe. And there's no pretence in it either.[8]

Sarratt makes no distinction between poetic language and poetic form. The rough and stupid fellows may not have aspired to write poetry, but their letters were no doubt written in what Fussell has called "Great War rhetoric"[9]—a style at best heroic, at worst maudlin, embodying a continuing reference to, perhaps a yearning for, traditional significance. This "high" diction, which dominated the writing of the early stages of the war, attempted to make sense of it through received perceptions.

Before the conflict was very old, however, certain authors identified a discrepancy between the events of the war and the capability of poetry, as they understood it, to realize the war; the realities of this war did not lend themselves to heroic and consoling verse. For some writers, at least, this meant that they were silenced, robbed of a voice. Colin Russell, Sylvia Thompson's hero in *The Hounds of Spring,* writes: "You ask me whether I have done any more poetry. I haven't much heart or soul for such things. I hadn't written anything since 1914 until the other day, when I wrote some verses and tore them up. They were ugly, broken things; and poetry should be born to strength and beauty—both of which seem very far away."[10] The only subjects available to him were "filth and horror and futility"; Mrs. Chase, his correspondent, had hoped that he would immortalize "courage, patience, wonderful endurance and sacrifice." It is a pity that Colin tore his poetry up. The "ugly, broken things" sound as if they might have won a place in the anthologies of war poetry current today. But Colin is no more willing (or no more able) to reconceptualize the role of poetry than Mrs. Chase is. Both remain true to the conventional understanding of the form. The difference between them lies not in what is the proper subject of verse but in their knowledge of the facts of the war.

It may be appropriate here to digress a little and consider why (*pace* Colin) the characteristic form for men's writing during the war was verse and for women's, prose. Both sexes used all available modes, but in each case the best work was achieved largely within one. I would suggest that it is because what men were writing constituted a *redefinition* and a *reevaluation* of what war can be, whereas what women were writing was a *definition* and *evaluation* of what the war meant to them. The situation the troops found themselves in was unprecedented, but that is not the same as saying that soldiers entered the war without historical and literary preconceptions and referents. To capture the way they were deceived by the present reality, they drew upon a deep mine of poetic imagery and myth (Fussell writes with profound insight on this subject in his chapter "Oh What a Literary War") and by reference and reworking found a resonant voice implicit in their sense of betrayal by the past. Women, on the other hand, were by and large carving out new territory as writers, writing a new chapter in their literary lives.[11] They did not require a mode that facilitated retrospective comparison; they required the flexibility of prose to range across and knit together their various contemporary experiences.

= Modernism =

Bernard Bergonzi summarizes the impact of the collision of events and their literary realization when he writes that the "literary records of the Great War can be seen as a series of attempts to evolve a response that would have some degree of adequacy to the unparalleled situation in which the writers were involved."[12] The "unparalleled situation" is the new, industrialized, mass trench warfare, the experience of which, it is argued, led to the abandonment of traditional rhetoric. One might be able to make out some sort of case for individual women writers needing to evolve a response to experiences that were equal in horror to those of the soldiers: writers like Mary Borden, say, with her four years of nursing near the front. Vera Brittain, also a nurse, writes of her own experience in the war zone and compares her situation with that of frontline troops: "Certainly no Angels of Mons were watching over Etaples, or they would not have allowed mutilated men and exhausted women to be further oppressed by the series of nocturnal air-raids which for over a month supplied the camps beside the railway with periodic intimations of the less pleasing characteristics of a front-line trench."[13] But there is a great difference between being "mutilated" and feeling "exhausted," and, besides, such women were in the minority.

To understand why the canon of World War I literature was originally, and still remains, a masculine one, it is important to recognize the overwhelming cultural significance and mythic resonance that were given to those war experiences available only to men (essentially combat and every horror that is subsumed in the phrase "trench warfare") and the lack of value that was afforded the social, personal, and spiritual dislocation and the anguish of loss that women shared with men. The significance of the struggle for woman suffrage was equally underrated. I cannot compare men's and women's individual pain, but, whatever the specific experience, its literary realization required the development of appropriate language and form from all narrators. Women had experienced a revolutionary alteration in their social and working lives, in their perceptions of themselves, their strengths, and their duties, and it was as unparalleled as soldiers' experiences. But because women did not partake of the specific elements perceived as being formative for men writers, the changes that occurred in their writing went unacknowledged and unrecognized. Borden's description of her experiences as "the rest that can never be written" suggests an equal failure of traditional rhetoric.[14] If it was solely the experience of combat that forced the new ways of writing, women must have continued to depend on conventional forms, having remained yoked to pious platitudes of style, excluded not merely from the canon of war writing but from modernism itself. That both of these premises are palpably untrue is clear from the examples of Borden, Woolf, and H. D. alone. Parfitt's argument for coexisting perceptions is closer to the truth than the oversimple argument that it was men's physical presence at the front that forced from them the new idioms necessary to realize the new perception.[15]

Writing about changes in the vocabulary that men found appropriate to the experiences they were undergoing, Eksteins says: "Traditional language and vocabulary were grossly inadequate, it seemed, to describe the trench experience. Words like *courage*, let alone *glory* and *heroism*, with their classical and romantic connotation, simply had no place in any accounts of what made soldiers stay and function in the trenches. Even basic descriptive nouns, like *attack, counterattack, sortie, wound,* and *shelling,* had lost all power to

capture reality."[16] He illustrates his point with a quotation from Roland Dorgeles, who wrote after the war that there are "grand words that don't sound
the same today as in 1914."[17] This is true, but before another myth becomes
fixed in the postwar consciousness, it is salutary to remind ourselves that
Hemingway did not declare that "abstract words such as glory, honor, courage, or hallow were obscene beside the concrete names of villages, the numbers of roads, the names of rivers, the numbers of regiments and the dates"[18]
until 11 years *after* Mary Borden had enunciated the bitter ironic modernist
understanding of the war in *The Forbidden Zone*, which she wrote between
1914 and 1918. For further evidence, we might also do well to look at contemporary women's verse: Catherine Reilly asserts, "Women were writing their
own protest poetry long before Owen and Sassoon."[19]

Elshtain argues that women's interpretations were different from men's
as far as they related to their different experiences: "men see edifying tales
of courage, duty, honor, glory as they engage in acts of protection and defense
and daring: heroic deed doing. Women see edifying stories of nobility, sacrifice, duty, quiet immortality as they engage in defensive acts of protection,
the nonheroics of taking-care-of."[20] But she neglects to recognize that both
sexes who knew the realities of this war were alike in their rejection of such
abstractions, and alike in undergoing revolutionary experiences that brought
revolutionary insight. In Temple Bailey's *The Tin Soldier*, Hilda says: " 'Men
are seeing things over there that they'll never see again. *And women are*' "
(emphasis added).[21] Both sexes would need to find appropriate forms to
express these unparalleled visions.

Elshtain underestimates the extent to which both men and women radi-
cally reassessed how they might realize in writing their social, political, and
cultural roles and attitudes. She fails to attach adequate significance to the
fact that in response to their interrogation of traditional models, women
writers were like men in employing all the different modes of response available at the time—from Fussell's "Great War rhetoric" to modernist irony.

As we saw at the beginning of this chapter, indicative vocabularies (referential and uncomprehending) can illustrate different perceptions (traditional
and modern). A typically self-conscious and complex piece of writing in Mary
Borden's *The Forbidden Zone* shows how both can be put to good use. In
"The Regiment" (whose vocabulary includes "immense . . . beautiful . . .
ineffably blue . . . superb castles . . . floating"), the shadows of the clouds
are described as being "flung like banners . . . over the green meadows and
fields of yellow corn" and the "smiling country" is enjoying itself as the "caress
of the wind sent shudders of pleasure through the corn and a fluttering delight
through the trees." Meanwhile, a "regiment was marching along the highroad
towards the town. . . . It looked like a shadow of a snake. . . . on a nearer view
the shadow became a column of hunchbacks, a herd of deformed creatures."[22]
Here a tone of objective disillusion is knowingly employed to sabotage the
sentiment of the initial description. Borden's new linguistic mode acknowledges

the perceived need for romantic imagery but displaces it with a style that displays soldiers as passive victims, deformed by an inhuman system. She shows contempt for traditional pieties; grotesque military absurdity implicitly undermines the romantic scene. Sordid perceptions and language deflate the rarefied imagery and break the rules of good taste.

The examples of different and changing vocabularies also serve as an indicator of the movement toward the wider concept of modernism. This omnibus term, loosely describing the dominant tendency of the arts in the first half of the twentieth century, reflects the impact of the cultural changes evident in the writings of Marx and Darwin, the psychology of Freud, and, perhaps, the anthropology of Sir James Frazer. Although diverse in its manifestations and its antecedents, modernism was recognized as representing "an abrupt break with all tradition. . . . The aim of five centuries of European effort . . . openly abandoned."[23] Technically marked by experimentation and innovation (succinctly categorized by Harold Rosenberg as the "tradition of the new"), it promotes discontinuity, rejects common experiences of reality, notions of causality, and traditional concepts of the wholeness of individual character. Modernist writing suggests a cultural crisis: language awry, cultural cohesion lost, perception fragmented and multiplied.

Writers who attempt to discuss the salient features of modernism, from Harry Levin and Frank Kermode to David Lodge and Julia Kristeva, agree that both form and style are characterized by sharp and sudden changes, a constant breaking up of the logical order of words; modernist techniques use reversal, surprise, and allusion with no apparent reference point. If the war was not modernism's source, the war contributed to its forms and eccentricities of style, its innovations constituting a subconscious reflection of the disorder and destruction experienced on the western front. It may be seen at its clearest in poetry. Richard Aldington, writer, poet, and soldier, wrote an ostensibly mild poem—"In the Tube"—describing a journey on an underground train; the conclusion, however, is unexpectedly violent and combative:

> Antagonism,
> Disgust,
> Immediate antipathy,
> Cut my brain, as a sharp dry reed
> Cuts a finger.
>
> I surprise the same thought
> In the brasslike eyes:
>
> "What right have you to live?"[24]

This poem, published in the *Egoist* in 1915, was followed on the same page by a poem by H. D. entitled "Mid-Day," which begins:

The light beats upon me.
I am startled—
A split leaf rustles on the paved floor.

I am anguished—defeated.

The devastation of the war is hardly concealed. The works published in the *Egoist* during wartime (which we have come to regard as forming the backbone of modernism) speak to the excesses of war on every page.[25]

Although elements of the modernist style can be found prior to the war, it was during the war that writers embraced modernism as the form in which they could make concrete their experience of disjunction and fragmentation. The modernist's freedom from realism, traditional genre, and form became associated with notions of cultural apocalypse and disaster. Offering a more sophisticated interpretation of the position propounded by critics such as Bergonzi, Malcolm Bradbury writes that "Many critics have seen the war as . . . the apocalypse that leads the way into Modernism, as violation, intrusion, wound, the source of psychic anxiety [and] generational instability."[26] By employing a longer perspective, Eksteins is able to offer a more subtle understanding of the role of the war in literary history; he writes that it "acted as a veritable exhortation to the revolutionary renewal for which the *prewar* avant-garde had striven" (emphasis added).[27]

May Sinclair, author of *The Tree of Heaven*, embodies women's engagement with the compelling issues of the early part of the century. As a novelist, suffragette, and wartime ambulance driver, she was involved in three contemporary arenas characterized by great conflict: modern art, woman suffrage, and the Great War. Longenbach points out that in *The Tree of Heaven* it is almost impossible to separate the battle for woman suffrage, the conflicts of modern art, and the war in the trenches.[28] It describes not only the "vortex of revolutionary Art" but also the "vortex of the fighting Suffrage women."[29] Both are "swept without a sound into the immense vortex of the War," each movement part of "the immense Vortex of the young century. If you had youth and life in you, you were in revolt."[30] All three conspired to change the face of modern culture. The most important historiographically, however, was the Great War, which quickly became the *apparent* stimulus for social and artistic revolution. This perception led to what we might summarily characterize as the "combat" explanation of the origins of modernism, and its development was subsequently to provide a basis for ignoring women's contribution to the canon.

The modernist novel shows two related preoccupations: firstly a sense of nihilistic disorder behind the ordered surface of life and reality, and secondly the representation of inward states of consciousness. Both elements are evident in women's war writing. The first, disorder, often appears as a lack of comprehension. In "The Captive Balloon," Mary Borden writes of "the motor cars of the army, the limousines, and the touring cars and the motor lorries and the ambulances," which become "monsters" that "have all gone wrong."[31] The unadorned refusal to explain in "all gone wrong" indicates a massive attitudinal change toward subject. Here Borden tries to cope with the enormity of the war experience through a bafflingly bald statement. It is as if she is conflating the military manner (reducing descriptions to simple statements, to bare objective accounts that omit individual suffering) with the incomprehension of the participant. There is a sense of powerlessness inherent in modern warfare that was experienced by a whole generation— the men who fought in the trenches and the women who accepted military discipline.

Likewise, Borden's "The City in the Desert" is a story that insists on *not* explaining[32]:

> The earth is a greased slide, tilted up and shaking. And the men who built this place knew evidently that there was danger of the face of the earth itself slipping—for look over there on that hill-side and that one—they've tied the earth down with wire. You see those intersecting bands of wire, looking like a field of tangled iron weeds and iron thistles? That is evidently to keep the mud from slipping away. . . . a secret place, vast, spread out, bare but secret; and some strange industry, some dreadful trade is evidently being carried on here in the wet desert, where a flood has passed and another flood will come.[33]

This is something more than a lack of comprehension. The writer here disassociates herself from understanding: "*the men* who built this place knew *evidently*" something she does not. The wire "is *evidently* to keep the mud from slipping away," but what the reality is cannot be understood. It is a "secret," a "strange industry," a "dreadful trade." The passage continues: "The workers have a curious apprehensive look with their big secretive bundles. They may be smugglers. Certainly some shameful merchandise is being smuggled in here from the shore that you say is not the shore of the sea. If the booming noise beyond the hills were the roar of waves breaking, one would say that these old men were gangs of beachcombers, bringing up bundles of wreckage."[34]

Eksteins writes that "As the purpose of the war became more abstract," it became "less amenable to conventional imagery."[35] We can find evidence of the rejection of convention being played out here by Borden. Only if the old world were real and its received perceptions functional—"They *may* be smugglers . . . *If* the booming noise . . . *were* the roar of waves"—would understanding be possible—"one would say that." But it is not. Even the implied listener denies it: "you say [it] is not the shore of the sea." And what is being described itself now refuses to allow explanation. Earlier the place had been described as "secret"; here the bundles themselves are "secretive." The witness is not only uncomprehending, but excluded.

The lack of explanation in such pieces is buttressed by a refusal to create coherence out of those elements that do function according to traditional means of perception. The use of seemingly incompatible elements mirrors directly what Parfitt, speaking of all novels coming out of the war, called "a marked tendency to fragmentation, to books frankly offered as records of moments and aspects of war experience."[36] He argues that this tendency runs parallel to the stylistic changes already identified: "the writer's linguistic register tends to work towards fragmentation, the writing becoming abrupt, with sharp variations of register, jerky transmissions, and even hectic inventiveness—these all reducing the possibilities of coherence and increasing the chances of uncertainties of tone and stance."[37]

A simple example of the relationship between fragmentation and coherence comes from Dorothy Canfield's *Home Fires in France*. Like Borden's *Forbidden Zone,* Canfield's book mixes fiction and reminiscence; its publisher's note is worth quoting in full:

> This book is *fiction* written in France out of a life-long *familiarity* with the French and two years' intense *experience* in war work in France. It is *a true setting-forth* of personalities and *experiences,* French and American, under the influence of war. *It tells what the war has done* to the French people at home. In a recent letter, the author said, "What I write is about such very *well-known conditions to us* that it is hard to remember that it may be *fresh to you,* but it is *so far short of the actual conditions that it seems pretty pale,* after all." (emphasis added)[38]

The complexities and ambiguities with regard to truth and fiction, and the difficulties of rendering conditions real to those who have not experienced them, are clear. Canfield's comparative lack of literary sophistication is evident, however, in the fact that, unlike Borden, she relies on traditional coherence, achieving a picture of war experiences through the connecting factors that accumulate in the sketches and stories that make up *Home Fires in France,* especially the plight of the modern woman faced with the barbarism of war (whose central location is "The Refugee" and "A Little Kansas Leaven") and the love of the land and the determination to restore it (apparent in "Notes from a French Village in the War Zone," "The First Time After," and the short story "The Permissionnaire," with its epigraph, "What was in the ground, alive, they could not kill").[39]

Canfield allows understanding to grow throughout the book. "The Permissionnaire" contains seemingly simple references to "the old walled garden" and to family ties to the village: "where he had lived for thirty four years,—where he had lived for hundreds of years."[40] Though the hero's sense of loss at the destruction of his home is clearly documented in the story itself, its true significance rests on a previous documentary section, "Notes from a French Village in the War Zone." It is only there that we read of "a thousand years of really sociable community life. . . . the close-knit communal organization of a French settlement"; of "an earthly Paradise of green; an old, old, garden with superb nut-trees, great flowering bushes, a bit of grass, golden graveled paths, and high old gray walls"; of gardens "gleaming, burnished, and ordered, with high old trees near the house"; of "the green, secluded peace of the walled-in garden." Similar references are also developed later.[41]

The refusal to explain, the fragmentation, and what Parfitt calls the "uncertainties of tone" are in reality the most appropriate means available to express an unacceptable truth. In the preface to *The Forbidden Zone*, Borden calls the book a "collection of fragments. . . . To those who find these impressions confused, I would say that they are fragments of a great confusion. Any attempt to reduce them to order would require artifice on my part and would falsify them."[42] This explanation—strangely but quite properly—is echoed by women critics today. Elshtain appears almost to be referring to Borden in her assessment of the effect of war and the rumors of war on her own childhood. She says that the "narrative in this chapter is purposely episodic, fractured . . . because it was the only way for me to remain faithful to my material."[43]

Borden presents us not only with a refusal to explain but with a refusal to *understand*: a refusal that suggests the ghastliness of the object of the incomprehension and the understanding. She realizes, too, that in the final analysis this refusal does not obscure the truth but makes it "unbearably plain": "I have dared to dedicate these pages to the Poilus who passed through our hands during the war, because I believe they would recognise the dimmed reality reflected in these pictures."[44]

Mary Borden has sophisticated means of conveying dawning comprehension. "The City in the Desert," which stresses incomprehension ("Down where? How do I know. I'm lost. I've lost my way"), describes men with "heavy brown bundles swinging between them. . . . Those heavy brown packages that are carried back and forth, up and down, from shed to shed, those inert lumps cannot be men."[45] It is not until the next sketch, "Conspiracy," that the explanation—that wounded men are wrapped in brown blankets—appears: "The stretchers slide out of the mouths of the ambulances with the men on them. The men cannot move. They are carried into a shed, unclean bundles, very heavy, covered with brown blankets." "Conspiracy" further advances the submerged narrative and describes the medical processes performed on the wounded, but in terms that are simultaneously mystical and negative: "We conspire against his right to die. We experiment with his bones, his muscles, his sinews, his blood. We dig into the yawning mouths of his wounds. Helpless openings, they let us into the secret places of his body. We plunge deep into his body. We make discoveries within his body.

To the shame of the havoc of his limbs we add the insult of our curiosity and the curse of our purpose, the purpose to remake him."[46]

It is only the next story, "Paraphernalia," that identifies the surgical procedures: "You finger the glass syringes exquisitely and pick up the fine needles easily with slender pincers and with the glass beads posed neatly on your rosy finger tips you saw them with tiny saws. . . . you rub his grey flesh with the stained scrap of cotton and stick the needle deep into his side."[47] Note also how the contrast between the violation of the body of the wounded and the control of the invasive nursing staff indicated in "Conspiracy" is extended in the contrasts here between the nurses' attractive competence ("exquisitely . . . fine needles . . . easily . . . slender pincers . . . neatly . . . rosy finger tips") and the sordid object of its attention ("grey flesh . . . stained scrap"). The (mis)quotation above, however, exaggerates the degree of understanding permitted since the last sentence is in reality a question: "*Why* do you rub his grey flesh with the stained scrap of cotton and stick the needle deep into his side? *Why* do you do it?" (emphasis added). Thus Borden establishes a pattern underlying the seemingly unconnected stories and sketches of *The Forbidden Zone*, a pattern of hesitantly growing comprehension, which is in constant conflict with her stated incomprehension, incomprehension that masks a refusal to understand, that tries to evade even worse experience, even partial understanding.

Incomprehension is often accompanied by a pervading sense of dehumanization. The soldiers are no longer men. The war itself is the vital element; the people, its victims, are automata. At the beginning of Borden's "Belgium" the Belgian people are dehumanized, mere abstractions only partially personified; it is the war that is given a voice, the trenches that bleed, the enemy who bites. Similarly, the reduction of human beings to inert objects in the factory system of a field hospital is expressed by Ellen La Motte in what has been called "a strikingly modern prose of flat repetition"[48]: "From the operating room they are brought into the wards, these bandaged heaps from the operating tables, these heaps that once were men. The clean beds of the ward are turned back to receive them, to receive the motionless, bandaged heaps that are lifted, shoved, or rolled from the stretchers to the beds."[49]

The lack of emotion in such prosaic writing is the correlative of the mechanical process it describes, exhibiting participation in what Glover characterizes as "descriptive detail which contributes to an expansive, sometimes unstable, realism."[50] Although he was describing a new literary tone that he felt was required to cope with the reality and perception of war as experienced by men, it was clearly required by women too.

In Borden's "Moonlight" we meet a completely dehumanized nurse:

She is no longer a woman. She is dead already, just as I am—really dead, past resurrection. Her heart is dead. She killed it. She couldn't bear to feel it jumping in her side when Life, the sick animal, choked and rattled in her arms. Her ears are deaf; she deafened them. She could not bear to hear Life crying and mewing. She is blind so that she cannot see the torn parts of men she must handle. Blind, deaf, dead—she is strong, efficient, fit to consort with gods and demons— a machine inhabited by the ghost of a woman—soulless, past redeeming, just as I am—just as I will be.[51]

As we have seen so often in this study, unsophisticated women writers who cannot be described in any way as avant-garde share similar strategies for writing about the war with modernists such as Borden. A tone similar to that in the passage above—inhuman and mechanical—is found, for example, in Mary Hamilton's *Three against Fate*. The heroine describes her mental state as being:

> like a gramophone sound-box: the little needle went round and round the disc, on a path one could not follow, and made this fearsome racket, but the record never came to an end, the spring never ran down, there was no stopping the noise. She had tried every way she could think of, and none of them worked.
>
> Perhaps, however, she had not been able to try hard enough, because it had taken all the strength of will and all the self-control she could summon merely to go on looking like a real person, and talking like a real person to other people. It had seemed somehow enormously important that they should not realize that she was not real any more.[52]

In 1949 Frederick J. Hoffman declared that a "sense of violation is present in each of the principal works of American war literature,"[53] and the "psychic wound" of the World War I veteran entered the literary vocabulary. The vulnerability of Borden's nurse and Hamilton's heroine shares this sense of violation. Claire Tylee would also include in this category the protagonist of Rose Macaulay's *Non-Combatants and Others,* Alix Sandomir, whose physically "crippled body manifests the incapacity of her nature to meet the demands of war-time society."[54] I would suggest that it is her mental state that is the more characteristic element, since mental damage more frequently represents the common vulnerability of the times. Macaulay describes Alix as "a broken, nerve-wracked, frightened child," and the words "broken" and "nerve-wracked" carry resonance of shell shock.[55] Even in a novel like *Mrs. Dalloway,* in which male and female experiences of the war (as represented by Septimus Warren Smith and Mrs. Dalloway) are kept distinct by keeping the characters physically apart, the narrative moves inexorably toward a final sense of their communion, which is achieved through their common vulnerability.

═ Inward States of Consciousness ═

During the war years and immediately afterward, the modernist writer's need to realize an anguished response to the experience of war became inseparable from the need to reveal inward states of consciousness. Eksteins speaks only of men when he writes that this "disequilibrium between the experience of the war and the subsequent response to it meant that the war, in its most important sense, as a social, political, and, foremost, existential problem, was relegated to the realm of the unconscious or, more precisely, to that of the consciously repressed,"[56] but the repression was found in both men's and women's writing. It encompassed an almost schizophrenic response of duality and of conflicting visions, and it included an awareness of the irrational and the workings of the unconscious mind made concrete in prose that rejected rational exposition in favor of stream of consciousness.[57]

Both intellectual and popular women writers felt the need for innovations to allow them to capture the unconscious and/or what was consciously repressed. In *Three against Fate,* for example, the heroine's mind moves in one paragraph from the flowers in her room to the men at the front:

> the sweet peas seemed to darken, to go brown, to go black. They were not flowers any more: they were leaves, rotting leaves, fallen and lying in great heaps under a pallid sky . . . and, as then, a ray of chilly sunlight came—through trees; for, somehow, she was out of doors now, in a wood . . . —and fell full on the purplish brown of the heaped-up leaves. And they took on a ruddy tinge, a tinge of blood, and stirred. Ah, they were not really leaves: they were the dead bodies of uncounted young men, trampled and corrupting at her feet. For miles and miles, those were the leaves with which the soil of Europe was being enriched. She gazed at them in mounting terror, seeing here an arm, there a leg, there a mangled, bleeding body, there a smashed disfigured face. The whole mass surged before her as though these were not corpses, but men still suffering, indescribably, abandoned and deserted in their agony. . . . she was held by that dark surging mass, from which there now rose sounds that filled her ears as well as her eyes with horror and even infected her nostrils. That dank smell was not the earth: it was the stench of death and decomposition.[58]

The transitional moments are signaled quite blatantly: the flowers "seemed" to darken until they "were not flowers any more: they were leaves." With the introduction of death and decay and an intimation that this may refer to soldiers (the movement is from "rotting" to "fallen and lying . . . under a pallid sky") comes another heavy directional indication: "somehow, she was out of doors." And so on throughout the passage: Hamilton, as though afraid of her "inventiveness," explains to the reader how the passage should be read.

Woolf is far more sophisticated in *Jacob's Room*, but the response of the unconscious mind to the war remains the subject. Jacob's mother is woken at night by the sounds of gunfire in France: "Again, far away, she heard the dull sound, as if nocturnal women were beating great carpets. There was Morty lost, and Seabrook dead; her sons fighting for their country. But were the chickens safe? Was that someone moving downstairs? Rebecca with the toothache? No. The nocturnal women were beating great carpets. Her hens shifted slightly on their perches."[59]

This famously interpretable passage at the end of the novel has much to offer in the way of understanding how allusiveness can reveal the nature—and the imaginative power—of the unconscious and of repressed thought. The war is captured initially in the sound of the guns, a "dull sound, as if nocturnal women were beating great carpets." This is a domestic image, which simultaneously announces the gender of the thinker, women's deflected connection with the war and their complicity in it, and above all its incomprehensibility. Quickly, however, the attitude appropriate to a patriotic mother is conjured up to provide a conventionally proper response—"Morty lost, and Seabrook dead; her sons fighting for their country." But this will not serve; it triggers a mother's transferred anguish—"But were the chickens safe?" The pain of this thought suggests an entirely new possibility, a hope that perhaps something else wakened her. Perhaps the war does not exist?— "Was that someone moving downstairs? Rebecca with the toothache?" Alas, the answer is "No." The passage moves toward its conclusion by returning to women's guilt and incomprehension—"nocturnal women . . . beating great carpets." The edginess and oblique nature of this response are beautifully captured in a final retreat to domestic concerns that simultaneously embodies and represses her anguish—"Her hens shifted slightly on their perches." Here is an implicit picture of a divided self, required to respond, incapable of response, in which the failure to find an appropriate mode of understanding is embodied in indirection.

Rebecca West's *The Return of the Soldier* provides an interesting reversal of the pattern employed by Woolf. At the end of the novel, when Capt. Chris Baldry, the soldier of the novel's title, is suffering from shell shock and amnesia, the three women in his life combine forces to reduce him to normality and return him to the front and almost certain death. But the leaden use of technical terms (" 'His *unconscious self* is refusing to let him resume his relations with his normal life. . . . what's the *suppressed wish* of which it's the *manifestation*? [Hypnotism only] releases the memory of a *dissociated personality* which can't be related . . . to the *waking personality*' " [emphasis added][60]) cannot create as subtle a portrait of the disassociated modern self as Woolf's allusive style.

One might have expected that Woolf's description of Septimus Warren

Smith's shell-shocked condition ("The world wavered and quivered and threatened to burst into flames") would of itself have ensured *Mrs. Dalloway* a place in the canon of war literature. Is its exclusion at least in part prompted by Woolf's allusiveness, her approach from the margins? Is the literary manner that has served women writers so well for so long in this case a factor in their exclusion? *Mrs. Dalloway*, set some five years after the conclusion of the war, does not suggest that any way can be found of accommodating the experience of the war (Septimus Warren Smith commits suicide), but at its conclusion the novel does allow Clarissa Dalloway to contemplate his death directly ("She felt somehow very like him—the young man who had killed himself)" and to return to her party.[61] Although Smith's defining moment is his suicide and Mrs. Dalloway's is her party, the reader should beware of automatically attributing more significance to the former. To Mrs. Dalloway, bringing people together is a vocation:

> What she liked was simply life. . . . [her parties were] an offering . . . .
> But could any man understand what she meant . . . about life? She
> could not imagine Peter or Richard taking the trouble to give a party
> for no reason whatever. . . . Here was So-and-so in South Kensington;
> someone up in Bayswater; and someone else, say, in Mayfair. And
> she felt quite continuously a sense of their existence; and she felt
> what a waste; and she felt what a pity; and she felt if only they could
> be brought together; so she did it. And it was an offering; to combine,
> to create. . . . it was her gift. . . . After that, how unbelievable death
> was![62]

Through Septimus Warren Smith and Mrs. Dalloway, Woolf is realizing the disjunction caused by the war.[63] Accepting the distinctness of their separate experiences, she is allowing woman's stronger hold on life to be victorious. The apparently trivial, feminine celebration of her party enables Mrs. Dalloway to face the perpetual threat of loss and death. It may also have unfairly excluded her author from serious critical consideration as a writer about the war.

Related to this disqualification may be women writers' use of gender-specific referents. Mabel Daggett writes of women who have received military decorations: "all of these women with their war jewellery for splendid service, are women like you and me. But yesterday, and they might have been pleased with a string of beads to wind about a white throat." Writing about the proliferation of wartime documents and passes, she says, "I give [the officer] my photograph. You always have to do that. Photographs that are duplicates of the one on your passport you must carry by the dozen. You have to leave them like visiting cards with gentlemen in khaki all over Europe."[64] Mildred Aldrich extends this mode of comprehension when she employs specifically domestic imagery. In describing a soldier as being "covered with dust from his head to his heels. I could have written his name on him anywhere,"[65] she is using her own experience to understand an alien situation. And Mary Borden uses a domestic comparison in exactly the same way, though to a grimmer end:

> Just as you send your clothes to the laundry and mend them when they come back, so we send our men to the trenches and mend them when they come back again. You send your socks and your shirts again and again to the laundry, and you sew up the tears and clip the ravelled edges again and again just as many times as they will stand it. And then you throw them away. And we send our men to the war again and again, just as long as they will stand it; just until they are dead, and then we throw them into the ground.[66]

Women's ability to realize their understanding through gender-specific imagery is an element in the reliance on allusiveness, on indirection, on writing from the margins that can still be found today. In Isabel Colegate's 1981 novel, *The Shooting Party,* the autumn of 1913 is considered as the prelude to the tragedy about to burst upon Europe through the story of a shoot that fully presages the coming slaughter, but does not directly confront it. Similarly with Radclyffe Hall: "His whole body looked pitifully soiled but resigned, and Alan could feel its profound desolation. For seeing him thus, was to know that Karl Heinrich realized in some dim way that he was dying, and that he had not yet made friends with death—perhaps because he was still so young and had been very full of the joy of living."[67]

This passage appears to offer a poignant moment on a battlefield and, indeed, within the metaphorical construct of the story, that is what it is. In terms of the plot, however, Karl Heinrich is a London cat, poisoned in a wave of anti-German feeling against his German owner, and about to be put out of his misery.[68] The story charts the impact of anti-German feeling on a maladroit and clumsy spinster, Fräulein Schwartz, who is in London teaching her mother tongue to the English; in this context the war is realistically discussed openly by her fellow lodgers. The action centers on the cat, and although in his own small way he is a casualty of the war, by no stretch of the imagination can the story be said to focus on the military aspect of the conflict. Until, that is, one comes to the central passage quoted above, when the story turns in on itself to reveal the true result of the lodgers' passionate prejudices. Once this central point has been understood, it comes as no surprise to the reader that Fräulein Schwartz kills herself.

Hall thus shares with Woolf and Colegate a sophisticated use of indirection, circling around the topic, appearing to avoid it, only to suck the reader further into confrontation with the impact of war. Commenting on this phenomenon, Higonnet suggests its cause: "The most powerful of women's writings about the war rely on indirection, or writing 'slant.' . . . there is a resemblance between women's writing and the devices of internal (and external) exile. . . . women's writing about war uses indirect techniques to evoke the experience of . . . forbidden subjects."[69]

The reference to exile suggests that it was because of women's political impotence that they could be forbidden from confronting some questions directly. But the examples from Hall, Woolf, and Colegate all clearly signal that war is their true subject; that indirection is rather a means of achieving an analytic discussion of the impact of the war that does not run the danger of being lost in descriptions of the physical horror of the war itself. Women writers do not attempt to describe combat, but indirection is neither imposed on them by their marginality nor used by them a means of avoidance.

Radclyffe Hall offers an individual slant on gender-specific perception. Every "decent instinct of courage" that Stephen Gordon, the heroine of *The Well of Loneliness,* has inherited, "all that was male in her make-up," is frustrated at the outset of the war since she can act as neither man nor woman: "She felt appalled at the realisation of her own grotesqueness; she was nothing but a freak abandoned on a kind of no-man's-land at this moment of splendid national endeavour. England was calling her men into battle, her women to the bedsides of the wounded and dying, and between the two chivalrous, surging forces, she, Stephen, might well be crushed out of existence." Eventually, however, England has need of even her for war work, and from women like herself who have "crept out of [their holes] and come into the daylight. . . . a battalion was formed in those terrible years that would never again be completely disbanded."[70]

Hall's short story "Miss Ogilvy Finds Herself" does not reflect the optimism about the continuance of the communal spirit described in *The Well of Loneliness.* After forming her ambulance unit, Miss Ogilvy "found herself quite at her ease, for many another of her kind was in London doing excellent work for the nation. . . . asserting their right to serve, asserting their claim to attention." In France, "she lived in a kind of blissful illusion; appalling reality lay on all sides and yet she managed to live in illusion." On her return to civilian life, however, she becomes desperate about her situation and reverts just before her death to an earlier life as a prehistoric male hunter! Even she is surprised by this turn of events: " 'Is it shell-shock?' she muttered incredulously. 'I wonder, can it be shell-shock?' "[71]

It would be no more correct to see Hall's response to the war as specifically lesbian than it would be to understand the homoerotic nature of the poetry of the war as a reflection of homosexuality among the troops.[72] Hall's sexuality may allow her to present the most clear example of the war acting as a stimulus to women to question their gender-determined roles, but she is by no means alone in such questioning. Pamela Hinkson takes an equally challenging, and pessimistic, tone in her novel *The Ladies' Road.* (Now, more than half a century later, it is perhaps necessary to remind ourselves of the echoes of rebellion that came from Hinkson's reference to the Chemin des

Dames, where in April 1917 the French command launched the disastrous and futile offensives that led to widespread mutinies among the troops.) Hinkson's young heroine Stella has no direction in her postwar life: "she faltered, staring at a road before her that seemed to lead nowhere—the Ladies' Road." Later, ironically regendering the world in which she will have to live after the war, Stella concludes that she "must live always in No Man's Land left by the War with a country on either side that was not hers,"[73] thus tragically employing the metaphor for her postwar existence with which Hall's Stephen had begun the war. In all cases, within one person, whether it is Stephen, Miss Ogilvy, or Stella, there lies the dissonance between the perceived experiences of the sexes.

As we saw in the first chapter of this study, the events of the Great War not only had "a very different meaning for men and women" but "were in fact very different for men and women."[74] This conjunction of meaning and event deserves further attention. Mary Borden offers a useful example of the relationship between men and women, between events and meaning, in her sketch "The Square":

> The little women of the town are busy . . . they have children with them. Some lead children by the hand, others are big with children yet unborn. But all the women are busy. They ignore the motors; they do not see the fine scowling generals, nor the strained excited faces. . . . They do not even wonder what is in the ambulances. They are too busy. They scurry across to the shops, instinctively dodging, and come out again with bundles; they talk to each other a little without smiling; they stare in front of them; they are staring at life; they are thinking about the business of living.
>
> On Saturdays they put up their booths on the cobble stones and hold their market. The motors have to go round another way on market days. There is no room in the square for the generals, nor for the dying men in the ambulances. The women are there. They buy and sell their saucepans and their linen and their spools of thread and their fowls and their flowers; they bargain and they clatter; they provide for their houses and their children; they give oranges to their children, and put away their coppers in their pockets.
>
> As for the men on the stretchers inside the smart ambulances . . . they do not know about the women in the square. They cannot hear their chattering, nor see the children sucking oranges; they can see nothing and hear nothing of the life that is going on in the square; they are lying on their backs in the dark canvas bellies of the ambulances, staring at death. They do not know that on Saturday mornings their road does not lie through the big bright square because the little women of the town are busy with their market.[75]

The women's constant activity is emphasized; they are "busy . . . are big with children yet unborn . . . are busy . . . busy . . . are staring at life; they are thinking about the business of living . . . they provide . . . are busy." By contrast, the men's role is negative; they "cannot hear . . . nor see . . . can see nothing and hear nothing of the life that is going on in the square; they are lying on their backs . . . staring at death. They do not know."

The conceptual and geographic meeting point of the men's and women's worlds is the square. Here the women—and life—hold sway for at least one day a week. "They ignore the motors . . . The motors have to go round another way on market days. There is no room in the square . . . The women are there . . . [The men] do not know that on Saturday mornings their road does not lie through the big bright square because the little women of the town are busy with their market." Most important, there is no communication between the two worlds. The women ignore the motors, do not see the generals, don't wonder what is in the ambulances. On market day, there is no room for the generals or the dying soldiers, who in turn know nothing of the women.

How far does this passage reflect what Gilbert calls "different meaning[s?]" Or is it only that the "events were in fact very different for men and women?" Borden, quite properly, makes it impossible to separate the two. The women are busy with life, the men with death; but the women are busy with domestic matters, with trivia. Their role may be life enhancing, yet they seem pitiless in their preoccupations as they ignore the men's suffering. They are the conquerors here, excluding men from "the big bright square." The events *are* different; the meanings *are* different; the two facts combine to create mutual lack of recognition. The reality is the metaphor. Such different perceptions mean that women's writing cannot fit smoothly into a canon that has been shaped exclusively by men's experiences.

The apparently pitiless detachment from men's suffering that Borden displays can also be found in Muriel Spark's short story "The First Year of My Life": "the German Spring Offensive had started before my morning feed. . . . On all the world's fighting fronts the men killed in action or dead of wounds numbered 8,538,315 and the warriors wounded and maimed were 21,219,452. With these figures in mind I sat up in my high chair and banged my spoon on the table." But again the true emphasis is less on a lack of compassion and more on the importance of ensuring that life continues— the baby is only preparing itself, as much as is possible, for the exigencies of being alive: "it was plain I had been born into a bad moment in the history of the world." Being omniscient, as it is claimed all babies are, it can travel to the trenches, and it knows their beastliness: "sheer blood, mud, dismembered bodies, blistered crashes, hectic flashes of light in the night skies, explosion, total terror. . . . Generally, I preferred the Western Front where one got the true state of affairs. It was essential to know the worst, blood and explosions and all, for one had to be prepared, as the boy scouts said." It is these experiences—this knowledge of "the true state of affairs"—which ensure that the baby's first smile occurs on hearing a family friend quote Herbert

Asquith's remarks in the House of Commons immediately after the war: " 'All things have become new. In this great cleansing and purging it has been the privilege of our country to play her part.' "[76]

Hamilton charts the process by which women came to share such hard-won understanding. She begins by stressing her characters' different perceptions:

> "Harold: tell me one thing. You haven't found someone else you care for?"
>
>> As she spoke, it sounded idiotic: her heart thumped in her throat as he looked at her on that, for a minute, with an expression she could not fathom. Then, suddenly, he laughed. His laugh was dreadful. It died. There was silence. He looked away. When his voice came at last, it seemed to reach here over a great distance: it was low, queerly muted, gentle:
>> "Poor little Jean! Is that all you know about it?"
>> A flush of bitter shame rose in her cheeks; she had a feeling of childishness: of talking to someone who had passed into a mode of existence beyond her imagination's range. She was answered: and ashamed.[77]

But before long Jean has come, via an entirely different route from his, to a position and knowledge similar to his: "Yes: now, she *knew* what he meant: then, she had not understood." Before long the essential changes wrought by the war are clear; she "shuddered as this thought came to her; in her own veins ran the subtle pervasive poison of war, which made death seem desirable."[78]

Tylee argues that men and women shared:

> the cultural myths and the behavioral inhibitions of their society. They suffered equally from the repression of their memories of traumatic experiences, and from a common vulnerability to the myths of imperialism. Writing was a means of purging the memory of shock, of bitterness and pain, and of anger. Discovering the new ways of writing formed a way of exploring and rejecting the whole panoply of war-propaganda, especially the bombastic rhetoric that had supported it. Through writing both men and women tried to salvage something from all the destruction. It enabled them to recapture vivid excitement and lost happiness, which were grieved for. It was also a means to conceptualise the personal changes that had occurred, and to relate them to the wider society. And the enterprise of creating a book could be seen as the construction of a fitting memorial to the dead. It was a memorial women could erect as well as men.[79]

Tylee's essential argument—that men and women begin from the same shared culture, experience the same "shock . . . bitterness and pain . . . anger

... excitement ... happiness," and use writing to discover, explore, recapture, conceptualize, and relate—is supported by any analysis of writing about the war; this makes it ever more unjust that women's war writing has been excluded from the literary history of these years and from the canon of war writing. Her argument is echoed in Parfitt's comparison of Enid Bagnold and Philip Gibbs, which ends: "both writers touch one of the most important ways of seeing the First World War—as transformation, even apocalypse."[80] He is able to conflate transformation and apocalypse, but to many the apocalypse of the trenches was the only criterion. Even if they had accepted women's transformation, it would not have been enough.

Chapter 2 refers to Jon Glover's summary of the characteristics of World War I writing, which deserves to be quoted at length. He begins with an analysis of content, foregrounding: "the physical and moral education of individuals or groups as the various new worlds of war are revealed. Identifiable stages continually recur: recruitment and training, the journey to the front, initial battle experience. And then, usually horrifyingly, the appearance of the dead, the experience of injury, hospitals and nursing. . . . injury, treatment and what was for many a first ironically brutal sharing of physical contact between men and women. . . . The effort to kill and the struggle to save and survive are starkly witnessed."[81]

Glover then addresses what structures are characteristically employed to realize these experiences: "On the one hand we see the continuity and repetitiveness of each individual's experience, the dreary and harrowing progression from recruitment to almost certain injury or death. . . . On the other hand . . . [there is] the episodic, unorganized nature of even the semi-fictional works. So much of the experience of war highlighted unprepared moments of confrontation and hate but also pity, selflessness and moral growth. . . . brief unstructured events. . . . plotless but detailed stories."[82] How little of the above is *not* found in women's writing about the war!

I have argued that an examination of the language and mode that women employed to write about their war experiences shows them to have been under the same constraints as men—literary, perceptual, and cultural—and that this remains true even when the actual wartime experience being realized was entirely different. It is for these reasons that women's writings are eligible for inclusion in the canon of writing about the war, and that answer Parfitt when he describes "the problems of defining which novels should be included and which excluded. . . . At what point does a novel which takes account of the war become a novel *of* the war?. . . . Should novels which concentrate primarily upon aspects of the war's effect at home be included, or novels concerned with how the war shaped post-war life?"[83] The response must be a resounding yes.

Surely it is not only male prejudice that has led to the neglect of women's writing? There are three different, but complementary, explanations. The first is the simple equation of war writing with writing about combat. The second is the belief that the experience of combat alone forced into existence the characteristic modernist idiom that was nurtured by the war. The third is that there are characteristics of women's writing that caused them to be excluded from consideration. Higonnet reaches toward this conclusion when she writes that "wartime changes [in women's experiences] . . . were discursively encoded."[84] In this encoding, women's traditional tools (psychological insight, allusiveness, the analysis of the domestic) have worked to their disadvantage.

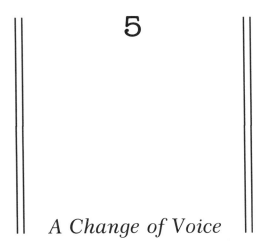

5

A Change of Voice

With the work of *his* hand, the words of *his* lips, *his* thoughts and the feelings of *his* heart, [the artist] identifies *himself* with this war drama, yet in the very depths of *him* he recoils.
   —John Galsworthy, *A Sheaf* (emphasis added)

Yet unity exists, despite the divisions in this "women's voice."
   —Judith Kazantzis, Preface, *Scars on My Heart*

THE WIDE RANGE OF WOMEN'S WARTIME EXPERIENCES MAKES it impossible to discuss the literary voice they adopted in a simple way. They were Land Girls, munitions workers, and nurses; they assumed men's jobs as police officers, bank tellers, and tram conductors. They served the cause in England, Belgium, France, and Serbia; their attitude might be patriotic, pacifist, cynical, or jingoist. Their writing took the form of novels, short stories, verse, memoirs, diaries, plays, sketches, and polemics.

   It is certainly true that the war acted as a stimulus to their writing.

Despite the fact that women writers hardly ever appear in bibliographies on the subject,[1] they wrote about their experiences constantly. Indeed, it would not be going too far to say that they found inspiration in the war. Gilbert claims that "a number of women writers . . . felt that . . . their art had been subtly strengthened, or at least strangely inspired, by the deaths and defeats of male contemporaries."[2] She quotes Vera Brittain, who noted that when her fiancé Roland Leighton was killed, ". . . his mother began to write, in semi-fictional form, a memoir of his life . . ." and that she herself was filled " . . . with longing to write a book about Roland. . . ."[3] Clearly, one motive for writing was to create a fitting memorial for the dead, to make sense of the short span of life they had been granted, and to capture in print something of the essence of those who had died so that they would not be completely lost to those they had left behind. But it is possible to identify another motive, which is just as strong.

═══ Participating in the War ═══

Before Roland's death, Brittain had little understanding of the effect war could have on women: "I was still too young to realise how much vicarious excitement the War provided for frustrated women cut off from vision and opportunity in small provincial towns. . . ." Significantly, she describes her Oxford tutor as a woman who ". . . was beginning to desire some occupation less detached from the War than the coaching of immature females. A year or so afterwards she escaped from Oxford to war-work in Serbia and Salonika."[4] The words "less detached," "immature," and "escaped" are telling. For some women, at least, the war was seen to offer opportunities for commitment, personal growth, and escape from civilian conventions and constraints.

Brittain also offers a darker insight into the role the war played in women's psyches, however, arguing that the need to share in the patriotic response, to be part of an overwhelmingly emotional, national commitment, led some women to assume the traditional wartime role of sufferer when they need not have done so: ". . . the deliberate contemplation of horror and agony might strangely compensate a thwarted nature for the very real grief of having no one at the front for whom to grieve."[5] Brittain's aperçu finds an echo in H. D.'s mystic statement that "the war was my husband."[6] Gilbert comments that: "at the very least, if the war was not her husband, it was her muse—as it was Woolf's, Mansfield's, Wharton's, and many other women's."[7]

There are complexities here that deserve our attention. What are the ways in which suffering can compensate? How can an object that the writer finds repugnant also inspire? Campton, the artist protagonist of Edith Wharton's A Son at the Front, expresses the ambivalence he feels at being an artist during the war—but not a war artist—in these words: "his artist's vision had been strangely unsettled. Sometimes . . . he saw nothing: the material world, which had always tugged at him with a thousand hands, vanished and left him in a void. Then again . . . he saw everything, saw it too clearly, in all its superfluous and negligible reality. . . . If ever there came a time for art to interpret the war . . . the day was not yet; the world in which men lived at present was one in which the word 'art' had lost its meaning."[8]

But for the reader there is a secondary contradiction that exists alongside and compounds the character's ambivalence. The passage quoted above occurs in a novel that is itself attempting through "art" to "interpret the war." It is significant that it is a woman author, who by the act of creation implicitly endorses the possibility of art interpreting the war, who put these negative thoughts into the mind of a man, and a man who finds himself forced by the war into the marginal position traditionally held by women in peacetime— inactive, uninvolved, at home, watching others (his son, in this instance) take an active role in historic events. In direct contrast, the war allowed women access to—in some cases forced them unwilling into—*participation*. Participation not in warfare itself, but in public life, in significant sacrifice, in the national emotion. Sharon Ouditt comments that the desire of some women, like Brittain's tutor, "to be at the site of death was seen to be equivalent to being at the heart of life. It was, effectively, an entry into history."[9] For women who had no vote, this was a seductive prospect, even, as Brittain suggests, for those for whom the only participation was through suffering.

Gertrude Stein, in a work that is more autobiographical than fictional, also speaks through the imagined voice of another, but this time the voice is that of a woman, her companion, Alice B. Toklas. Stein has Toklas describe her (Stein's) war work, visiting American and French troops and the wounded, and its effect on her writing. It "was during these long trips that she began writing a great deal again. The landscape, the strange life stimulated her."[10] Not long afterwards she describes the inspiring landscape:

> Soon we came to the battle-fields and the line of trenches of both sides. To anyone who has not seen it as it was then it is impossible to imagine it. It was not terrifying it was strange. We were used to ruined houses and even ruined towns but this was different. It was a landscape. And it belonged to no country.
>
> I remember hearing a french nurse once say and the only thing she did say of the front was, c'est un paysage passionant, an absorbing landscape. And that is what it was as we saw it. It was strange. Camouflage, huts, everything was there. It was wet and dark and there were a few people, one did not know whether they were chinamen or europeans.[11]

Three elements in this landscape are worthy of further consideration: the strangeness and the difference; the statelessness nature of the place that results in the nationalities of the inhabitants being uncertain; and the emotional intensity it arouses—although translated as "absorbing," the word "passionant" pervades this passage with the English sense of "passionate." This is a land that exists outside the known world; here things are camouflaged and here anyone may be (or may become) anything. Seen in this light, the war offers women not only the opportunity for passionate participation but also for some the opportunity to inhabit a topsy-turvy world, a world turned upside down, in which all options are open to them.

Women's regular inclusion of domestic material in their war writing has already been noted (see chapter 2), as has their use of gender-specific comparisons, which are also often domestic (see chapter 4). In light of the inspiration offered to women writers by wartime opportunities for participation, by a world of apparently unrestricted options, and by the consequent redefinition of self, it may seem perverse that they maintained explicit contact with the world to which they had traditionally been restricted. It will now be necessary to look further at this phenomenon.

In the following passage, Gertrude Atherton writes of two women writers who remained in France throughout the war and who fled before the Germans who ransacked their homes. Her deep subject, underlying the surface concern with the behavior of the Germans, is the importance of the domestic life in wartime, the importance of recounting the war on that front, and the importance of women recording their own history truthfully.

> I think it was early in 1915 that Madame Waddington wrote in *Scribner's Magazine* a description of her son's chateau as it was after the Germans had evacuated it. . . . Madame Huard, in her book *My Home on the Field of Honor*, is franker than most of the current historians have dared to be, and the conditions which she too found when she returned after the German retreat may be regarded as the prototype of the disgraceful and disgusting state in which these lovely country homes of the French were left; not by lawless German soldiers but by officers of the first rank.[12]

This reference to authenticity was at the heart of women's writing and of the voice they chose to employ; it was the authenticity of their war.

Mildred Aldrich's books of wartime letters contain progressively more and more about her "beasties," who include Argus, an Airedale dog who does not live very long, soon followed by a big black poodle called Dick and a kitten who "was evidently lost during the emigration."[13] Although the latter was "known to all [the] neighbours as 'the Grand Duc de Huiry,' " she names him Khaki; they are later joined, briefly, by another cat, "a dear little fluffy, half angora, which I named Garibaldi." Aldrich's choice of this subject is not random. Her correspondent has obviously voiced a complaint regarding the topics she had previously written about, and Aldrich replies, somewhat petulantly: "Evidently mine of the Fourth of July did not please you. Evidently you don't like my politics or my philosophy, or my 'deadly parallels,' or any of my thoughts about the present and future of my native land. Destroy the letter. Forget it, and we'll talk of other things, and, to take a big jump—Did you ever keep cats?" The entirety of this letter (18 September 1915) then continues the saga of her pets, concluding, "I cannot send you letters full of stirring adventures. I don't have any. I can't write you dramatic things about the war. It is not dramatic here."[14]

We may assume from this that what she had been requested to describe were the traditional subjects of war writing: adventure, heroics, combat. Seen in this light, Aldrich's insistence on writing only about domestic events (and those not even human-interest stories) takes on a more deliberate aspect. The importance of this episode is emphasized by its being referred to a second time more than 18 months later in *The Peak of the Load* (18 May 1917), in a passage that again introduces an entire letter dealing only with her pets:

> [A]lthough I have nothing much to write about, I am going to try to make a letter. Everything in the world is still—but though we hear no sound of cannon, I have the thought of it always with me. It is more persistent than the poor.
>
> I have been looking over some of your letters, and I find that . . . I have never got to telling you about anything in the beastie line, except cats—and you got that, you remember because you were nasty about my efforts to "Wake up the States," which had been hardly less successful at that time than dear Lord Roberts' great "Wake Up, England!"[15]

As she comments wryly at its conclusion: "You can't call this a war letter, can you?"[16] Despite her correspondent's preconceptions and desires, and her own earlier ritual obeisance to traditional subjects, by now Aldrich is stubbornly insisting on keeping to what she perceived to be the truth of her experiences.

Nor is this pattern unknown in men's writing. Eksteins claims that "Material concerns—references to meals, cigarettes, clothes, equipment, and a host of such irritants as weather and vermin—dominated; emotions rarely transcended trite sentimentality; and the war as a whole was usually described in platitudes."[17]

Another American journalist, Mabel Daggett, was younger and more outspoken than her compatriot and thus perhaps found it easier to abandon conventional literary tropes. This may explain why she is able to come somewhat closer to articulating the difference of vision that is implicit in the conflict between what Aldrich has been asked to do and what she is willing to do. As a reporter, Daggett is even more preoccupied with the contrast between what she wants to write and what is expected of her:

> It is the martial mind that I must meet. A Press Bureau, you see, is prepared to pass promptly propaganda on the battles of the Somme.

But dare one risk say a pamphlet on the breast feeding of infants? Propaganda about the rising value of a baby! Dear, dear, it might, for all a man could tell, be treason, seditious material calculated to give aid and comfort to the enemy! Already to my inquiries about maternity measures in Paris, have I not been answered suspiciously: "But why do you ask? This matter it is not of the war."

My emasculated data at last are ready for review by *le chef du service de la presse*.[18]

On first reading, Mabel Daggett appears to be arguing that the martial mind understands only the importance of battles, and that babies and breast feeding are outside its ken—such information *"might,* for all *a man* could tell,"* be seditious. In light of the uncertainty Daggett thus signals, however, we should hesitate before accepting the ready explanation that to allow information about childcare to be included in war reporting might give aid and comfort to the enemy. The real danger is that its inclusion challenges the assumption that wars are men's affair, men's property. The underlying truth of the matter lies more securely in the subsequent exclamation, " 'This matter it is not of the war.' " And by "the war" we are to understand combat and the ultimate sacrifice, which both justify and define men. This is what is behind Daggett's ironic comments, her destabilizing use of "material" (which has all the resonance of *"materiel"*) and her reference to "emasculated data."

But even Daggett encodes her understanding; she is not willing to attack the military openly. In the face of men's suffering, it was not possible for women to challenge their assumption directly at the time ("To question those values is to question the Sacrifice itself—impossible"[19]); indeed it is difficult for a woman analyst to articulate Daggett's perception even now. Olive Dent, writing of a common argument during her service as a VAD, explains: "the heated opposition we always have from the boys when we sometimes say what we often passionately feel, that we nurses would gladly and proudly go as far up the line as we could be useful, and that it is our duty to take the same risks of being killed, wounded, or maimed as they. But chivalry, it seems, is not yet dead, and this subject remains the only one on which the boys contradict and oppose us."[20]

Chivalry is a generous explanation for women's exclusion—no less than one would expect from women rendered unable to argue their point by the overwhelming pity they felt for what men were suffering at the time. It does not mean, however, that later generations of women should refrain from pointing out the injustice of such attitudes and the dangers inherent in them.

Although the writing that came out of the Great War has come to be understood as breaking the mold and cutting itself free from earlier heroic models, it was identical to the old in its exclusion of women. Judith Kazantzis suggests that this attitude comes from "something quite deep in the patriarchal mind . . . which generates a general lack of interest in women's wartime experience, including the endlessly repeated tragic one of bereavement."[21] The characteristic records of the Great War were to perpetuate such beliefs as the *exclusive* comradeship of the trenches, the *incalculable* tragic waste of those who died, the *incommunicability* of the experience. The words themselves are redolent of the division of experience of those "who had been there" (who were men) and those who had not (who were women). It became an act of postwar piety to nurture such myths and to give the writing that embodied them cultural pride of place. But in doing so, our culture was deprived of a full understanding of its true literary history. Claire Tylee describes this male monopoly: it "has not only excluded women's memories. It has given support to the idea that the war is a men's affair." But Tylee also identifies a danger in terms of our intellectual history: "It has also obscured the significance of what happened to women for our understanding of social and cultural change. The battlefront is not the only theatre of war."[22] In other words, the full significance and meaning of the impact of war on society have been minimized by their limited literary realization. "One of the most important myths we have inherited from the Great War was that the experience of battle was incommunicable; you had to have been there. 'Those That Had Been There' formed an exclusive, quasi-mystical fellowship. Exclusive, naturally, of women. . . . women could not sympathetically share in the understanding of what the experience had been like."[23]

This belief was held by the soldiers themselves during the war. Their poetry in particular is characterized by its emphasis on capturing the moment of experience rather than revealing or interpreting it to others. It will typically, in its address, imply the understanding of other initiates. It does not articulate the experience to noncombatants, since they would in any case be incapable of understanding what the soldiers had been through. If it is directed at civilians, it will be to berate them for their lack of understanding. It is a form of address that does not permit dialogue. Nor does it extend recognition to other experiences.

In the memoir of one of the very few women who served (and was wounded) in the war, we find a telling example of the domestic illuminating the military. Waking up the morning after a difficult and bitterly cold retreat with Serbian wounded in an ox wagon, Flora Sandes and her companions

> found to our sorrow that the recruit had not put the cork back in my water bottle, and the rest of the brandy had upset, as had also a bottle of raspberry syrup which the Kid set great store by. I once upset a pot of gooseberry jam in a small motor-car, and it permeated everything until I had to take the car to a garage to be washed, and go and take a bath myself before I could get rid of it; but it was not a patch in the way of stickiness to a pot of raspberry syrup let loose in a jolting wagon, and we were very glad to get out at daybreak, after eight hours' travelling, to walk a bit to stretch our legs, and also to wipe off some of the stickiness with some grass.[24]

For her the domestic, rather than detracting from the military, illuminates it and places it within a comprehensible and communicable framework.

Claire Tylee writes that we do "not read the works of West, Woolf or Hall in order to gain any knowledge of conditions on the Western Front or the responses of the 'Other Nation' to those conditions." But in doing so she does not imply that the contribution those writers make to our understanding of the impact of the war is in any way insignificant; it is rather that they are writing another war (one that even today remains in danger of being forgotten). The women's war—even that of a woman soldier—is one that cannot be understood in only military terms. This fact should not invalidate what they wrote, however. Their books "are every bit as important to an understanding of modern consciousness as are, for instance, Richard Aldington's *Death of a Hero* or the verse of Siegfried Sassoon—*women's* consciousness, that is."[25]

But it was those who participated in combat who determined how the war was encoded in the annals of history. For Olive Dent, understanding begins when she realizes that the men she knows and the heroes of the past are identical: "And here we are living in the midst of history makers, men who have more than once taken part in deeds equalling and, on occasion, excelling that of Balaclava, and we readjust our notions of history makers, we correct our perspective, we humanize and individualize those makers of history. We realize that they were not men of super-human nerve, muscle and endurance." This perception leads her to consider their female counterparts: "We bring to mind *for the first time* the little, old-fashioned, girl-children . . . the grey-robed Puritan wives . . . the Victorian wives" (emphasis added), and she realizes that no one will speak for the experiences of their modern counterparts: "And when the standard histories of this war come to be written, no doubt they will be done by terribly efficient old gentlemen. . . . written in polysyllabic prose and in epic style."[26] For Dent, those who are taking part in historical deeds and those who will write the history in "public" prose that will ignore women's experiences in the war are one and the same: they are the "history makers."[27] Those who served in the trenches will be both actors *and* scribes, and as such they will become the only keepers of a new canon of war writing.

While I have argued that the war offered women the possibility of participation, it is true that they were excluded (Flora Sandes notwithstanding) from the soldiers' war. Thus the women who wrote about the Great War had to perform a different and complex double function; they were actors in their own war *and* spectators of the soldiers' war. In a book that is a stimulating attempt to put the Great War into its artistic and cultural context, but which, by accepting the definition of the war as an activity for men only, is doomed to be incomplete and consequently inaccurate, Eksteins writes of the importance of response: "the audience for the arts . . . is . . . an even more important source of evidence for cultural identity than the literary documents, artistic artifacts, or heroes themselves. The history of modern culture ought then to be as much a history of response as of challenge, an account of the reader as of the novel . . . of the spectator as of the actor."[28] If this is true, it means that the contribution of women writers to the definition of cultural identity, rather than being insignificant, is of particular importance.

= Writing the Women's War =

In reading women's war books, there is a constant sense of how important their authors felt their writing to be; how imperative it was that their testimony become public. Mildred Aldrich talks of the need for "writing out my adventures," although "for days at a time, I had no desire to see a pen."[29] Her wartime memoirs and short stories contain comments about writing and the act of story telling, about books and papers—even the documents and forms required by the military authorities assume significance. In *On the Edge of the War Zone* alone, Aldrich identifies passports, forms and registers, *permis de séjour, permis de sortir, sauf-conduits, carnets d'ètrangére, dossiers,* and *cartes d'identité*. A characteristically deflected commentary on the importance she feels should be attributed to such everyday documentation occurs when a passing reference to such "necessary [wartime] papers" triggers thoughts of "the proudest documents in the annals of the historic town."[30] The connection between the two is complicated: not only do the everyday papers lead her to think in terms of documents of record, but the latter are explicitly linked to the recording of history ("annals"). A further telling aspect of the tacit comparison she is making comes from the nature of the "proudest documents" themselves. They do not, as one might imagine, record heroic exploits but the measures taken for "the safety of the poor [and] the care of the wounded and the dead."[31] It is not difficult to decode this passage: civilians' papers are important evidence of the true experience of the war; they can serve as historical records as justly as more conventional accounts; and history itself ought to find a place for the achievements of noncombatants.

We may find another encoded analysis of the relationship between documentation, women's writing, and the validation of their perception of the war in Dorothy Canfield's sketch "Some Confused Impressions." In it she describes how two French refugees plead with her to assist them to obtain permission from the American forces to return to their village:

> "If Madame would only write on a piece of paper that we only want to go back to our home to take care of it—. . . . If Madame would only write on a piece of paper in their language that—"
>
> So I did it. I tore a fly-leaf out of a book lying in the heap of rubbish before the ruins of a bombarded house . . . and wrote "These are two brave old people, inhabitants of Villers-de-Petit, who wish to

go back there to work under shell-fire to save what they can of their own and their neighbours' crops. Theirs is the spirit that is keeping France alive."[32]

It is impossible not to read the repetition of the phrase "a piece of paper" through the eyes of a generation formed by World War II, but we should strive to understand it in its own terms. Only writing will enable the refugees to achieve their goal. Only writing may be able to bridge the gap between civilians, whose simple desire is to restore the land, and soldiers, who are implicated in its destruction. The passage not only connects soldiers with ruins, bombardment, and shell fire but, more significant, with the destruction of books. Only the woman writer can translate the refugees' request into English; but it is not only English that is meant by "their language"—it is the military language of the soldier. In granting their request, the narrator comments, " 'It probably won't do you a bit of good . . . but there it is for what it is worth.' . . . They went off trustfully, holding my foolish 'pass' in their hands."[33] In the "foolish pass" is summarized the woman war writer's attempt to mediate between the vision of the war held by the military mind and the truth of war as experienced by noncombatants. And Canfield was right—in the long term it didn't do a bit of good: the vision of the military mind has imposed itself on subsequent generations as the only truth of the war.

Women writers were not unaffected by the realization of their outsider status in the soldiers' war, and this often resulted in their writing having a hesitant, even apologetic, tone; simultaneously, however, the experience of the women's war was of vital importance to them and so had to be given a voice. Women's need to find ways in which their individual experiences could be made available to readers inevitably made first person narratives (whether documentary or fiction) the most important form: "first-person accounts, real or imagined . . . invite us to enter a war of words, to familiarize ourselves with the text and the texture of wartime experience."[34] The narrator as participant is as central a concept of women's writing as it is of men's.

History has chosen to ignore women's war and literary history, the literature of that war. The fact that women's writing rested on the belief that their experiences were significant and capable of communication has, of itself, been a causative factor in its neglect. And this can be seen even in such an otherwise perceptive and sympathetic critic as Peter Aichinger. He describes Edith Wharton and Willa Cather as writing "some of the more enduring works in the prowar category. The success of both these authors depends on their treatment of the effects of war on the personality of the individual rather than on their appreciation of the significance of the war."[35] Ignoring the simplistic and inaccurate relegation of Cather and Wharton to the "prowar category," the ultimately patronizing definition of their subject as nothing more than the "effects of war on the personality of the individual" is little more than a reworking of women's reputed inability to see beyond the personal; certainly they cannot be expected to appreciate the wider "significance of the war."[36] That Wharton and Cather may be attempting to realize something different was never considered.

Because they were writing as both actors and spectators, women were enabled to communicate, if only for a moment, a sense of the incommunicable. In Rose Macaulay's *Non-Combatants and Others,* Alix Sandomir is forced to face up to what the war means to her, and this must include some understanding of what it means to the soldiers. The moment is neatly encapsulated in her overhearing a convalescent cousin talking in his sleep, as he relives the nightmare of the trenches: "legs and arms and bits of men flying through the air."[37] Pamela Hinkson uses a similar image when Nancy Creagh overhears her son Guy—at home after being gassed—in his room. He is talking "to himself unintelligibly. She listened, holding her breath for a word, a clue that must help her. But she was shut outside as though he was a stranger speaking a strange tongue."[38] In sleep, as in combat, the men are in a world the women cannot enter; they are speaking an unknown language—a language designed to externalize the internal only in order to reveal its impenetrability, not to communicate, not to explain. Women writers respect the incommunicable nature of men's experience, but they need to recognize and express what they understand about it.

Why did women writers prioritize communication and explanation while so many men writers presupposed a certain understanding on the part of their audience? It is easy, but no less true for all that, to say that it is because women's experiences were generally less horrific and thus more communicable. But this does not constitute a sufficient explanation. The psychological trauma suffered by nurses who moved almost overnight from the genteel protection of a middle-class home to all the ghastliness of wartime nursing might well have resulted in a literature that presupposed an exclusivity equal to that found in men's writing.

Vera Brittain comments on the general "physical and psychological shock" the war inflicted on women, and she writes of the intense emotion nurses experienced at the first death among their patients, which she compares with ". . . the feeling of shock and impotent pity that had seized Roland when he found the first dead man from his platoon at the bottom of the trench." But it would get worse: "After the Somme I had seen men without faces, without eyes, without limbs, men almost disembowelled, men with hideous truncated stumps of bodies . . ." and these horrors did not disappear from memory: ". . . War's repressions were already preparing their strange, neurotic revenge." Brittain was to continue to suffer ". . . those nightmare recapitulations of hospital sounds and sights of which other wartime nurses complained for two or three years" more.[39] And Mary Borden writes of "episodes that I cannot forget."[40] Ouditt suggests a further way in which such experiences would affect women: "The trauma of the daily experience of nursing—especially on the Western Front—destabilised for some women what had come to be their way of identifying themselves. The complexity and ambiguity of these women's experiences [were] largely owing to the violent clash between the conservative ideologies that enabled them to get out to the war and the failure of those ideologies to mediate or account for the trauma that later beset them."[41]

Despite these traumas, what we find is a style that gives priority to communication and explanation. And this is true even of the employment of the incommunicable and incomprehension by such modernist writers as Borden (see chapter 4). The sophisticated sequences of *The Forbidden Zone* take as their *subject* the very nature of the incommunicable, just as much as do Macaulay and Hinkson. This is very different from assuming an exclusive audience of "those who have been there."

When Ruth Farnam writes of her experiences in Serbia, she appears to be addressing almost explicitly those who have not been there:

> I listened and wanted to help, but as I had no training at all, had never even been with sick people and had practically never seen blood, I did not feel very competent. . . . We had a man whose head had been broken by a piece of shell and he was, in consequence, completely paralyzed. There was some growth on his back . . . which had to be removed and I had to hold him in my arms to keep him in the proper position during the operation.
>
> We had no anaesthetic. . . . The poor fellow was in a fearful state of nerves as he lay in my arms, screaming, but unable to move a muscle.
>
> The feeling of his bare body on my bare arms, his screams, his breath, the odour of blood and the sound of the knife softly passing through the flesh were at last too much for me. I managed to stand it until the operation was over and then I went into the open air and was deathly sick.[42]

Edith Wharton suggests that noncombatants who suffered bereavement in the war saw "the horror face-to-face" and thus could understand the combatants.[43] Flora Sandes compares her early nursing experience with her later ability to respond to her charges after having shared their travail as a soldier:

> Before, when I had been working in the hospitals, and I used to ask the men where it hurt them, I had often been rather puzzled at the general reply of the new arrivals, "Sve me boli" ("Everything hurts me") . . . but in these days I learnt to understand perfectly what they meant by it, when you seem to be nothing but one pain from the crown of your aching head to the soles of your blistered feet, and I thought it was a very good thing that the next time I was working in a military hospital I should be able to enter into my patient's feelings.[44]

Other women also went more than half way toward understanding men's anguish, using their own pain to transcend the barrier between their war and that of the soldier: "Empathy between the sexes had to operate over . . . a dividing wasteland of experience. . . . Some cross it with triumph."[45]

The reason women do not address only those who have known their own pain and do not seek to exclude others from their experiences comes, perhaps, from the premium women came to give to their newfound maturity, development, and experience. Whatever pain they experienced, it meant that they were beginning to speak with authority. Women's writing of this time contains frequent references to maturity: "There are no French *girls* left— they are all women now"; "Definitely, she was now a woman, not a girl"; "Many, many things the girl of the Red Mill was learning these days. If they did not exactly age her, she felt that she could never again take life so thoughtlessly and lightly. Her girlhood was behind her; she was facing the verities of existence."[46] This is even true of the naïve Hinda Warlick in Wharton's *The Marne*, who early on in her time in France "appeared to think that Joan of Arc was a Revolutionary hero, who had been guillotined with Marie Antoinette for blowing up the Bastille [but who nevertheless]. . . . was ready and eager to explain France" to anyone who would listen. Before she returns to America, however, she has come not only to understand the French but to recognize her earlier ignorance: " 'Since I came to Europe, nearly a year ago, I've got to know the country they're dying for—and I understand why they mean to go on and on dying. . . . I know France now—and she's worth it! . . . I have to laugh now when I remember what I thought of France when I landed.' "[47]

Many of the quotations in the preceding paragraph come from American authors; they share a unique and specific point of reference—the American Civil War, which was also often used as a measure of national experience and maturity. Mildred Aldrich calls to mind her New England childhood: "I am old enough to remember well the days of our Civil War, when regiments of volunteers, with flying flags and bands of music, marched through our streets in Boston, on the way to the front. Crowds of stay-at-homes, throngs of women and children lined the sidewalks, shouting deliriously, and waving handkerchiefs, inspired by the marching soldiers, with guns on their shoulders, and the strains of martial music. . . . But this is quite different."[48]

Her range of reference here is quite traditional: the glamour of the forthcoming battle is captured in the volunteers, the flags, the music. At such an early stage (the letter is dated 10 August 1914), Aldrich simply asserts that this war will be different. Almost exactly three years later (14 August 1917) she can be more specific: she knows the effect of lists of casualties, repeated day after day in the press. It is interesting that she so disassociates herself from the heroic view of warfare that she implies it is her correspondent who has introduced the subject of the romantic trappings of battle: "I wonder if a full realization of the situation over here will ever come to you in the States. I don't yet see how it can. The ocean is wide. I know myself how difficult it is to arrive at an actual conception of a far-off disaster. But I suppose that, next year, when every day's newspaper will carry its list of casualties, you will feel quite different from what you do now, and have less taste for the sight of marching regiments and bands of music."[49]

Vera Brittain was 21 when the war began. She wrote throughout the war and was thus able, like Aldrich, to reflect on her own former attitudes. Explaining the inclusion in *Testament of Youth* of early (and now discarded) opinions, she writes: "The naive quotations from my youthful diary which I have used . . . are included in this book in order to give some idea of the effect of the War, with its stark disillusionments, its miseries unmitigated by polite disguise, upon the unsophisticated ingenue who 'grew up' (in a purely social sense) just before it broke out." Notice that she is not claiming that it was the war that forced her to grow up; she is making the more important point that the very notion of what constitutes being grown up has been changed by the experience of the war. In 1915, when she is still only 22, she will look back at her prewar self ". . . with the half-sorrowful, half-scornful indulgence that a middle-aged woman might feel when coming upon the relics of some youthful folly."[50] The weary tone of sad disillusionment has been hard bought.

Despite the fact that Mildred Aldrich was 40 years Brittain's senior (Aldrich was born in 1853, Brittain in 1893), she can on occasion write with a more youthful certainty. Though a noncombatant, she confidently asserts not only that she is right but that her correspondent will be converted to her point of view: "I am sorry that you find holes in my letters. It is your own fault. You do not see this war from my point of view *yet*—alas! But you will. Make a note of that. . . . You are going to come some day to the opinion that I hold."[51] Despite Aldrich's assured tone, I would not wish to suggest that other women writers (or even Aldrich herself on other occasions) always speak with such certainty. To say that women felt that they were gaining maturity is not to claim that every insight they gained is presented with confidence. It is not. But they felt a growing security in the knowledge that they are authorized to narrate the women's war, even if what they have to narrate is uncertainty or incomprehension.

In chapter 1 we saw how different women's experiences of the war were from men's. Chapter 2 argued that while women's choice of subject—both explicit and implicit—was capable of defining a different agenda, it also partook of an underlying similarity to men's writing. In chapter 3 we saw how, like their male counterparts, women writers chose and adapted the romance to meet their needs. In chapter 4 a consideration of women writers' relationship to and employment of the dominant literary mode was supported by an analysis of the language they used. So far in this chapter I have extended the analysis of women's writing to argue that three things contributed to women's profound need to speak: the opportunity for participation; an understanding of the significance of the right to narrate bestowed by the authority of the experiences of *their* war; and the implicit maturity these developments permitted. To understand the final element in women's response to the war it will be necessary now to look at how the voice they adopted, the conflated voice of actor *and* spectator, helped them to realize and articulate their vision.

== Actors and Spectators ==

To distinguish women's true voice, we should perhaps begin, as we have done so often in this study, by acknowledging the many similarities in style between men's and women's war writing. Vera Brittain is aware of the connection. She quotes from a letter to her mother, written after she has been in the war zone at Etaples:

> "Here," I wrote to my mother, exactly two years after the Battle of Loos, and *in language not so different from that used by Roland* to describe the preparations for the first of those large-scale massacres which appeared to be the only method of escape from trench warfare conceivable to the brilliant imagination of the Higher Command, "there has been the usual restless atmosphere of a great push—trains going backwards and forwards all day bringing wounded from the line or taking reinforcements to it; convoys coming in all night, evacuations to England and bugles going all the time; busy wards and a great moving of the staff from one ward to another. . ." (emphasis added)[52]

She knows that the style is similar because so was the experience.

Women could also adopt the jolly tone of good chaps, and in an even-handed way, too. Flora Sandes writes that the English Consul "was a perfect trump in the way he did his duty by stray English subjects and looked after their safety." Of her Serbian commander—"when I got to know him very well and had the privilege of being a soldier in his regiment, I found out that not only was he a sport, but one of the bravest soldiers and most chivalrous gentlemen anyone ever served under."[53] The latter quotation in particular captures the tone of respect and even devotion found in the reciprocal comments of some British troops and their officers.

When necessary, women writers can, like men, adopt the high diction. Mrs. Humphry Ward, writing in her book *Towards the Goal,* trumpets that "Wickedness and wrong will find their punishment, and the dark Hours now passing in the torch-race of time, will hand the light on to Hours of healing and of peace. But the dead return not."[54] Even Vera Brittain, hankering after her wartime months in Malta, calls it ". . . a shrine, the object of a pilgrimage, a fairy country which I know that I must see again before I die. . . . Come back, magic days! I was sorrowful, anxious, frustrated, lonely—but yet how vividly alive!"[55] This is the traditional rhetoric of patriotism and nostalgic sentiment that could be employed for elegies and inspirational verse or in referential prose that supported the war and the sacrifices it demanded. As we saw in chapter 4, it was available to capture women's vision in what is in effect a "transferred voice" from men's writing of the early years of the war.

And, like their male counterparts, women writers begin to feel embarrassed at what comes to seem the inappropriateness of such language. Eksteins writes, "In the letters and diaries of front soldiers, both volunteers and conscripts, there is less and less mention, as the war drags on, of the overall purpose of the war, the defense of civilization, and more and more reference to the individual's limited social horizons—his family, comrades, and regiment."[56] This attitude is clearly apparent in the embarrassment Mildred Aldrich feels at her correspondent's characterization of her description of a battle as "spectacular." She writes that "I am shocked to hear that I was spectacular. I did not mean to be. I apologize. Please imagine me very red in the face and feeling a little bit silly," and later she writes: "You must overlook my eloquence!"[57] In "Tish Does Her Bit" Mary Roberts Rinehart describes the means Tish employs to thwart what she wrongly thinks is Culver's intention to get married to save himself from being available for the draft (during this escapade her nephew manages to carry out his actual intention of enlisting); in an attempt to rouse the men's patriotism, Tish delivers "one of the most inspiring patriotic speeches I have ever heard. She spoke of our long tolerance, while the world waited. Then of the decision, and the call to arms. She said that the sons of the Nation were rising that day in their might. . . . It was at that time, we learned later, that the policeman . . . decided that Tish was insane."[58]

The second mode used by women—as by men—to set against the traditional and the referential is modern and fragmented; it foregrounds both authenticity and uncertainty through unreality and irony and is typically used to capture disillusionment and cynicism. Vera Brittain manages to capture in one passage the contrast between the flat monotonous prose of those in shock and the frenzied prose necessary to do justice to the cause of the condition. During frantic activity at Etaples in April 1918, she finds herself repeating, "The strain all along is very great," without knowing why these particular words have come to mind:

> "The strain all along," I repeated dully, "is very great . . . very great."
> What exactly did those words describe? The enemy within shelling
> distance—refugee Sisters crowding in with nerves all awry—bright
> moonlight, and aeroplanes carrying machine-guns—ambulance
> trains jolting noisily into the siding, all day, all night—gassed men
> on stretchers, clawing the air—dying men, reeking with mud and

foul green-stained bandages, shrieking and writhing in a grotesque travesty of manhood—dead men with fixed empty eyes and
shiny, yellow faces . . . Yes, perhaps the strain all along *had* been
very great . . .[59]

The irony of the stylistic contrast lies in the fact that the repeated phrase had
originally been that of her father describing mere domestic inconvenience.
Elshtain's comment on the irony employed by men and women in writing
about the war is apposite: "important, too, is the *ironic* spirit generated by
the disillusioned of the First World War. The ironist locates himself or herself
in the world in a way that mocks heroic words and action. The ironist knows
that war is not what it is cracked up to be."[60] The only difference from men's
writing is that the irony made available by the point of view adopted by
Brittain allows her to mock the domestic rather than the heroic, the strategies
of the home front rather than the western front.

Olive Dent's description of women's role in the war begins with what
is characteristically a man's sentimental view of those at home who need
defending; notice how the first two objects requiring protection are female:
"One looked at one's dear ones at home with a passion of over-mastering
love. One caught one's self looking at strangers in the street, on the bus, and
in the railway train,—at that worn little mother with the tired, trouble-
haunted eyes, the laughing girl-child with the soft rounded limbs, the croon-
ing baby with his whole, wondrous future before him. Who was to defend
them all?" But before long she has to adopt a more practical voice: "Defence
was the only consideration in the popular mind in those early August days.
And defence was a man's job and I, unfortunately, was a woman."[61]

Beyond the ability to employ the tone of men writers lies women writers'
characteristic ability to combine the two tones of participant and observer.
All Quiet on the Western Front concludes in the third person with the information that Paul Muller died in October 1918. Evadne Price, seeking as
always to mirror that book, also ends *"Not So Quiet . . ."* in the third person:
"Her soul died under a radiant silver moon in the spring of 1918 on the side
of a blood-spattered trench."[62] But notice how even here Price indicates
Smithy's role both as actor ("died") and spectator ("on the side").

Virginia Woolf provides the most sophisticated examples of the double
voice adopted by women to cope with writing about the war. At the time she
was writing *To the Lighthouse*, she entered the following comments in her
diary: "My theory being that the actual event practically does not exist. . . .
The method of writing smooth narration can't be right. . . . Why not invent
a new kind of play; as for instance: Woman thinks . . . / He does." Between
them these comments provide a running commentary on the novel that are
particularly apposite for the short section entitled "Time Passes." Elsewhere
in her diary she defined it as the "lyric portions of [the book, which] are
collected in the 10-year lapse and don't interfere with the text so much as

usual." It was, she wrote, "the most difficult abstract piece of writing—I have to give an empty house, no people's characters, the passage of time, all eyeless and featureless with nothing to cling to."[63] This pivotal section pictures the gradual decay of the house, the dark, the winds, the rain, the sea, the seasons—all taking their toll until the ravages of weather, time, and nature are opposed by the domestic care women employ against them; as the house becomes even more desolate in its silence, Mrs. McNab "came as directed to open all windows, and dust the bedrooms."[64]

Into this overwhelmingly elegiac mood, six bracketed passages are interpolated. The first, dealing with one character only, introduces a note both of continuity and of cessation: "[Here Mr. Carmichael, who was reading Virgil, blew out his candle. It was midnight]." Two pages later, in a passage in which two characters are mentioned, continuance appears to be threatened: "[Mr. Ramsay, stumbling along a passage one dark morning, stretched his arms out, but Mrs. Ramsay having died rather suddenly the night before, his arms, though stretched out, remained empty]." On first reading, the third section appears to righten the balance—"[Prue Ramsay, leaning on her father's arm, was given in marriage. What, people said, could have been more fitting? And, they added, how beautiful she looked!]"—but she too is leaving the house, and the movement away from the closed world of the family is emphasized by the intrusion of the wider concept of "people." The people are there again in the fourth insertion: "[Prue Ramsay died that summer in some illness connected with childbirth, which was indeed a tragedy, people said, everything, they said, had promised so well]." Notice here how the passage contains not only a conclusion ("Prue Ramsay died that summer") but the negation of a possibility for continuance ("childbirth"). In the next bracketed section the scene has become fully public, indeed historical; the people are now numbered and involved in the action: "[A shell exploded. Twenty or thirty young men were blown up in France, among them Andrew Ramsay, whose death, mercifully, was instantaneous]."[65] There is no continuity here—only death. The pattern of these interpolations (which are marked as intrusions in their being bracketed off from the rest of the text—"smooth narration can't be right"[66]) is one that leads toward ending and death, toward the collapse of the private and the invasion of the public and historical; death and the number of dead grow at the expense of the continuation of the family.

They are set within a chapter of 25 pages or so of lyrical desolation, which deals with the passage of 10 years in the life of the house. It is not difficult to relate the surrounding text to the bracketed sections. Near to the first passage, when guests are still welcome and where we have discovered continuity, we read that "the little airs mounted the staircase and nosed around bedroom doors. But here surely, they must cease. Whatever else may perish and disappear, what lies here is steadfast." Before the second, which tells of Mrs. Ramsay's death and Mr. Ramsay's search for her, "the little airs" have changed: "The nights now are full of wind and destruction . . . it is useless in such confusion to ask the night those questions as to what and why and wherefore?" Prue's marriage sits in a section that begins with an ominous tone, connected to her by its female nature—"The spring without a leaf to toss, bare and bright like a virgin fierce in her chastity, scornful in her purity, was laid out on fields wide-eyed and watchful and entirely careless on what was done or thought by the beholders." Although the passage that surrounds her death includes references to hope and to dreams—"the white earth itself seemed to declare (but if questioned at once to withdraw) that good triumphs, happiness prevails, order rules"—but the earth only seems to endorse this optimism, and if questioned withdraws at once. And the spring "veiled her eyes, averted her head, and among passing shadows and flights of small rain seemed to have taken upon her a knowledge of the sorrows of mankind."[67]

Given this evidence of a sympathetic relationship between surrounding text and bracketed inserts, we may expect to find significant commentary on Andrew Ramsay's death on the western front in the passage that surrounds it. What is happening in the house and on the beach? Before Andrew Ramsay's death, there came "ominous sounds like the measured blows of hammers dulled on felt, which, with their repeated shocks still further loosened the shawl and cracked the tea-cups. . . . a giant voice . . . shrieked so loud in its agony." The imagery is of gunfire, destruction, and pain. Afterward, there is "something out of harmony. . . . the silent apparition of an ashen-coloured ship . . . a purplish stain upon the bland surface of the sea as if something had boiled and bled." Nature saw men's "misery, his meanness, and his torture. That dream, of sharing, completing, of finding in solitude on the beach an answer, was then but a reflection in a mirror. . . . the mirror was broken."[68] The passage of time may have shaken the stability of the house, but the war has brought the family to the point of breakdown. It has threatened the dream of sharing, the house is in danger from its "repeated shocks."

The overall context of the full section is one in which women are charged with the task of defeating time. Woolf does not shrink from locating this process within "dailiness," within practical and humble measures, and it is the women who are successful.[69] It is they who enable the final section of the book to be written, who bring about the gradual postwar awakening of the house and make possible the visit to the lighthouse. The action (the event, which "practically does not exist," as Woolf wrote in her diary) is cramped into brackets, is minimized, shrunk, seen from outside. It is now the other: if "Woman thinks . . . / He does"; this section gives priority to thought and marginalizes the action. Woolf has established women's priorities (private, domestic, continuing) as the definitive touchstone against which men's actions and their public history are judged.

This distinction of subject is present in both the structure and the tone of "Time Passes." The continuity of the house, supported by the woman's work in it, is given the actor's voice; the events are given to the spectator. Woolf has addressed both the interior and the exterior. She has put the war at the center of a discussion of time, causation, and continuance. She has found a double voice that articulates its impact and honors the unsung continuity of women.

Woolf does not *argue* this point. Indeed, Ouditt describes Woolf's writings as performing "a radical critique of existing power structures while avoiding an agressive methodology. They are not confrontational."[70] A further, potentially more comprehensive explanation, however, is that the war itself was responsible for the fragmentation of the existing power structures. The women who observed the war saw it blow apart their known world, destroy the accepted limits of relationships, whether between persons or nations, and this legacy of the war provides the clearest explanation of the presuppositions of modern women's writing.

There remains one final bracketed section to consider: "[Mr. Carmichael brought out a volume of poems that spring, which had an unexpected success. The war, people said, had revived their interest in poetry]."[71] Surely a last ironic comment from Woolf that, despite her manner of achieving a narration of the women's war, she knows that it is the men who will create the record? She might have achieved a voice, but it will not be allowed to extend itself into the realm of the historical and the literary.

Joan Scott claims that "Women's experience . . . provides insight . . . into the discrepancy between domestic, private history and official, national history,"[72] a discrepancy nicely summarized in Canfield's title *Home Fires in France,* which contains within it a perceptive dissonance between the warlike "Fires in France" and the domestic "Home Fires." Domestic and private histories come as truthfully from women's experiences as those arising from the experiences of men writers, and are as much a part of national history. To write their history, women, "like men, drew upon existing cultural responses to make sense of their experiences."[73] It may be that despite a commonalty of experience, the dissonance that comes from reference to gender-specific cultural responses has meant that neither sex could hear what the other was saying.

A comparison of Helen Thomas's account of her husband's last departure for the front with his own reveals the differences in the man's and the woman's experience of the event and its realization in writing. She writes:

A thick mist hung everywhere and there was no sound except, far away in the valley, a train shunting. I stood at the gate watching him go; he turned back to wave until the mist and the hill hid him. I heard his old call coming up to me: "Coo-ee!" he called. "Coo-ee!" I answered, keeping my voice strong to call again. Again through the muffled air came his "Coo-ee." And again went my answer like an echo. "Coo-ee" came fainter next time with the hill between us, but my "Coo-ee" went out of my lungs strong to pierce to him as he strode away from me. "Coo-ee!" so faint now, it might be only my own call flung back from the thick air and muffling snow. I put my hands up to my mouth to make a trumpet, but no sound came. Panic seized me and I ran through the mist and snow to the top of the hill, and stood there a moment dumbly, with straining eyes and ears. There was nothing but the mist and the snow and the silence of death.

   Then with leaden feet which stumbled in a sudden darkness that overwhelmed me I groped my way back to the empty house.[74]

Edward Thomas was killed in France at the battle of Arras in April 1917. His diary for January 1917 recounts how he saw his last journey and suggests how difficult it is to find a simple basis for constructing an account of "difference." He writes:

   Up at 5. Very cold. Off at 6:30, men marching on frosty dark to station singing "Pack up your troubles in your old kitbag." The rotten song in the still dark brought one tear. No food or tea—freezing carriage. Southampton at 9:30, and there had to wait till dusk, walking up and down, watching ice-scattered water, gulls and dark wood beyond, or London Scottish playing improvised Rugger, or men dancing to concertina, in a great shed between railways and water. Smith and I got off for lunch after Horton and Capt. Lushington returned from theirs. Letter to Helen from "South Western Hotel." . . . Hung about till dark—the seagulls as light failed nearly floated instead of flying— then sailed at 7. . . . A tumbling crossing, but rested.[75]

The subject matter is contiguous—the misery of departure in the depths of winter; there is some sharing of mood. But the difference is striking. It is more than the fact that Helen Thomas writes with the knowledge of her husband's death (this excerpt comes at the end of a narrative that has been slowly gathering itself in dreadful anticipation). Or that they are using different forms (a memoir; a diary). The soldier's diary is of the moment; piling up impressions, keeping memories for later use. He is focused and other people appear only briefly; the entry is full of observation and detail, the only emotion is indirect: "The rotten song in the still dark brought one tear." She allows the emotion to permeate the entire scene ("mist . . . no sound . . . mist . . . hid . . . muffled . . . echo . . . fainter . . . pierce . . . away from me . . . faint . . . muffling . . . panic . . . mist . . . dumbly . . . nothing . . . mist"). She writes of his departure, but loads the scene with evidence of their relationship ("his old call"), her love for him ("*keeping* my voice strong to call again"), her fear of her loss ("silence of death . . . leaden . . . sudden darkness . . . empty house"). Actor *and* spectator, she implies the full horror of the woman's war she is experiencing while recognizing the horror of his, which she can only, hopelessly, despairingly, watch.

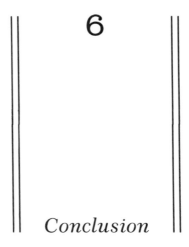

6

Conclusion

These four years have so much changed the whole aspect of life that it is not easy to say what one's literary tendencies will be when the war is over.

—Edith Wharton, quoted in R. W. B. Lewis,
Edith Wharton: A Biography

This book is to be neither an accusation nor a confession, and least of all an adventure, for death is not an adventure to those who stand face to face with it. It will try simply to tell of a generation of men who, even though they may have escaped its shells, were destroyed by the war.

—Erich Maria Remarque, prologue,
All Quiet on the Western Front

AND WHAT OF THE GENERATION OF WOMEN "WHO, EVEN though they may have escaped its shells, were destroyed by the war"?

Many were thinking about what the future would hold even before the war was over. In a letter dated 10 October 1917, Mildred Aldrich writes: "One thing I know, people who expect when this is over to come back to the France of before the war are going to be mightily disillusioned. The France of the old days is gone for ever. I believe that all over the world it will be the same. We none of us shall get back to that, but I have faith to believe that we are turning our faces towards something much better. If we are not, then all the great sacrifice has been in vain."[1] Aldrich moves smoothly in this passage from the national to the personal; the war had brought change in both arenas.

Temple Bailey's character Drusilla says that English women " 'are driving ambulances or making munitions. When the Tommies come marching home again they will find comrades, not clinging vines.' "[2] Gertrude Atherton spells this out in more detail: "never before have women done as much thinking for themselves as they are doing today. . . . they have been obliged to think for themselves, for thousands of helpless poor, for the men at the Front." And she is as optimistic about the outcome as Aldrich: before the war the American woman was "either an expensive toy or a mere household drudge, until years and experience give her freedom of spirit. This war will do more to liberate her than that mild social earthquake called the suffrage movement. . . . the passion of usefulness, the sense of dedication to a high cause, the necessary frequent suppression of self, stamp the soul with an impress that never can be obliterated."[3]

Equally hopeful, the outspoken American reporter Mabel Daggett predicts the rewards that women will receive: "The new democracy for which a world has taken up arms, for the first time since the history of civilization began, is going to be real democracy. There is a light that is breaking high behind all the battle lines! Look! There on the horizon in those letters of blood that promise of the newest freedom of all. When it is finished—the awful throes of this red agony in which a world is being reborn—there is going to be a place in the sun for women."[4]

Men would be held accountable for ensuring "a place in the sun for women," for making sure that a future society recognized their proper position. This was not to be a prize for their wartime services but in recognition of women's true strengths, which their war work had revealed. Turning her attention now to her European sisters, Atherton writes:

> there is persistent speculation as to what the thinking and the energetic women of Europe will do when this war is over, and how far men will help or hinder them. . . . the men in authority should not be permitted for a moment to forget, not the services of women in this terrible chapter of France's destiny, for that is a matter of course, as ever, but the marked capabilities women have shown when sud-

denly thrust into positions of authority. . . . That these women should be swept back into private life by the selfishness of men when the killing business is over, is . . . unthinkable.[5]

If justice is not freely offered, she says, it may have to be taken:

> It is probable that after this war is over the women of the belligerent nations will be given the franchise by the weary men that are left, if they choose to insist upon it. They have shown the same bravery, endurance, self-sacrifice, resource, and grim determination as the men. . . . never, prior to the Great War, was such an enormous body of women awake after the lethargic submission of centuries, and clamouring for their rights. Never before have millions of women been supporting themselves; never before had they even contemplated organization and direct political attack. . . . There is hardly any doubt that if this war lasts long enough women for the first time in the history of civilization will have it in them to seize one at least of the world's reins.[6]

The revolution so confidently predicted by these American writers will be wide-ranging, and men may have to accept a lower social status, perhaps working in future as maids of all work: "The truth of the matter is that there is a vast number of men of all races who are fit to be nothing but servants. . . . All 'men' are not real men by any means. They are not fitted to play a man's part in life, and many of the things they attempt are far better done by strong determined women. . . . I can conceive of a household where a well-trained man cooks, does the 'wash,' waits on table, sweeps, and . . . makes the bed without a wrinkle."[7]

In such a future, sexual relationships will be revolutionized. It has already begun in some countries: "The Frenchwomen in particular have forced men to deal with them as human beings and respect them as such, dissipating in some measure those mists of sex through which the Frenchman loves to stalk in search of the elusive . . . quarry"; and this will no doubt continue. Writing of what she assumes will be a typical marriage after the war, Atherton recognized that not every husband may wish to "accept his wife's enlarged circle and new interests after the war is over . . . but nothing is less likely than that she will rebuild the dam, recall the adventurous waters of her personality, empty her new brain cells, no matter how much she may continue to love her husband and children."[8]

As we now know, this brave new world was not to be. The interwar years were to see a clawing back of many of the rights, opportunities, and sexual freedoms gained by women during the war. Half a century later Joan Scott can take the story a little further and describe how opinions like Atherton's were successfully challenged as sexual mores were reestablished. The prewar status quo was reestablished because the relations between the sexes were argued to be "timeless, unchanging, outside social and political systems. The turmoil of politics is then depicted as an overturning of the natural order: men are weak and impotent, while women are strong, ugly, domineering, taking over public life, abandoning husbands and children. War is the ultimate disorder, the disruption of all previously established relationships, or the outcome of earlier instability. War is represented as a sexual disorder; peace thus implies a return to 'traditional' gender relationships, the familiar and natural order of families, men in public roles, women at home, and so on."[9]

Vera Brittain, watching the changing situation at the time, supports Scott's thesis and is able to give personal evidence of the profound ambivalence of the national response: ". . . on July 22nd, 1919, while a regular chorus of praise of women's war-work was accompanying their gradual replacement by men in every type of occupation, the House of Commons passed the Second Reading of the Sex Disqualification (Removal) Bill, with its comprehensive opening words: 'A person shall not be disqualified by sex or marriage from the exercise of any public function, or from being appointed to or holding any civil or judicial office or post, or from entering or assuming or carrying on any civil profession or vocation.' "[10]

But if genuine political change was not forthcoming, Brittain has a profound understanding that the war has completely changed her life. In amazement, she compares what before the war she had thought would be her future with what after the war she has actually become: "Had I been able to look into the future . . . I should have believed myself destined to die in the interval and waken again to quite another life. And such a fate was perhaps, after all, not so different from the one that actually befell me." She sees the change as personal, not as part of a national or social revolution. In her analysis, the difference between her pre- and postwar lives is equivalent to her death. What has died, what perhaps was never alive, is her youth. That is the void, the death, which cuts her off from her prewar self. "Dear Edward, shall we ever be young again, you and I? It doesn't seem much like it; the best years are gone already, and we've lost too much to stop being old, automatically, when the War stops—if it ever does. If it ever does!"[11]

Women writers came, like men, to accept that there was not going to be a bright new future for them. They belonged to a blighted and "condemned generation," trying to find a way of continuing its life. Those who survived were like ghosts at the feast, and equally unwanted: " 'I'm nothing but a piece of wartime wreckage, living on ingloriously in a world that doesn't want me!' Obviously it wasn't a popular thing to have been close to the War; patriots, especially of the female variety, were as much discredited in 1919 as in 1914 they had been honoured I reflected . . ."[12]

But those who survive cannot forget, and many chose not to forget. Vera Brittain continues this passage encapsulating the events that it has taken her almost 500 pages of the book to tell:

I reflected, *making no effort to shut out the series of pictures that passed insistently through my mind*—the dark, blurred spire of a Camberwell church at midnight—the *Britannic* lurching drunkenly through the golden, treacherous Archipelago—sun-drenched rocks and a telegram on a gorgeous May morning—Syracuse harbour and the plaintive notes of the "Last Post" testifying to heaven of the ravage of a storm—the German ward and the sharp grey features of a harmless little "enemy" dying in the sticky morass of his own blood—the Great Push and a gassed procession of burned, gruesome faces—the long stone corridor of St. Jude's where walked a ghost too dazed to feel the full fury of her own resentment—Millbank and the shattering guns announcing the Armistice. (emphasis added)[13]

How many others made "no effort to shut out the" memories? How many more tried but failed?

Once the war is over, the survivors remain in some way crippled by it. Their responses will be in some way impaired. Brittain writes that the knowledge of a coming separation ". . . renewed the feeling of sick inertia that came when wartime leave had ended and someone was returning to the front. In the depths of memory I knew that, for those of us who were now experienced and disillusioned, no parting would ever again have quite that quality of desolation and finality which overwhelms the moment of farewell to one's first love in early youth."[14]

Erich Maria Remarque knew that his book was primarily about the postwar generation. "*All Quiet on the Western Front* was not a book about the events of the war—it was not a memoir, much less a diary—but an angry declaration about the effects of the war on the young generation that lived through it."[15] Its spectacular success heralded a flood of books and other material dealing with the war, ushering in what came to be known as the publishing "war boom" of 1929–30. And what the postwar books would try to deal with was the question of the future. Again Vera Brittain offers the apposite comment. Toward the end of *Dark Tide,* she comments, "It's one's future, not one's past, that they really hide—those graves in France."[16]

Toward the end of *Testament of Youth,* Brittain wrestles with the question of whether there is any future for her. One thing she does know is that romantic love is no longer possible: ". . . those romantic hopes of late flowering, of postponed fulfilment, to which some of my contemporaries clung so pathetically, were merely a form of cowardly self-delusion in which women who had seen the destructive realities of War should know better than to indulge." But if she cannot make a life for herself, she may be allowing the war the final victory: "So long, I knew, as I remained unmarried I was merely a survivor from the past—that wartime past into which all those whom I loved best had disappeared. To marry would be to dissociate myself from that past, for marriage inevitably brought with it a future. . . ." Yet the necessary metamorphosis may be beyond her strength: "Could I, a wartime veteran, transform myself into a young wife and mother, and thereby give fate once more the power to hurt me . . . ?"[17] It is noticeable that in this question Brittain contrasts the phrase "wartime veteran," with its implicit masculinity, with the female "wife and mother." Not only will she be required to defy the "death" of her youth, but to change sex as well.

The double irony is that if she does defy the war, accept a new sexual identity, and assert her moral right to a future, she will also have to accept that the war has defeated her, because to do so she will have, finally and irrevocably, to bury her dead: "There remained now only the final and acute question of loyalty to the dead; of how far I and the other women of my generation who deliberately accepted a new series of emotional relationships thereby destroyed yet again the men who had once uncomplainingly died for them in the flesh."[18] To claim a future may be the hardest burden imposed on women by the war.

Mary Lee's novel "It's a Great War!" captures the flat, commonplace banality of the postwar world in prose that is redolent of drab domestic detail. This unemotional style has been defined as part of a postwar sexual reassessment. Alison Light writes that "something happened to middle-class femininity after the Great War which sees it taking on what had formally been regarded as distinctly masculine qualities: in particular the ethics of a code of self-control and a language of reticence whose many tones can be picked out in the writing and also in the construction of writing selves in the period."[19] On her return to America after the war, Lee's heroine does not expect to marry, but if she does the only man possible for her is Jerry. He chooses, however, someone who has not been destroyed by her war experiences. The book ends as follows:

> "You'd better marry Jerry, Anne!" laughed Randolph. "Give up your visions. It's the only way out!" Anne shook her head.
> "Why should I marry?" she said. . . .
> Still,—Why not? Life would be empty,—She stood, looking at the letter. . . . "I want you to be among the first to know, Anne . . ." Jerry engaged. . . . Life to begin again. . . . Life,—a glass of champagne, a plate of soup, and now, the soup grown cold . . .
> "Dinner'll be ready in ten minutes, dear." . . . Anne got up, strolled towards the old, red curtains, out on to the stairs . . . The third step would squeak . . . The bathroom, up there, shining, waiting . . . Clean towels . . . A hot bath . . . A lifetime of,—
> "Yes, dinner,—" Anne said . . . [20]

It would, of course, be foolish to suggest that only women had to discover the means to face the future. The process of understanding the full effects of the war was a task for the entire generation who survived it, and indeed for many future generations. "The casualty lists went on appearing for a long time after the Armistice—last spasms of Europe's severed arteries," wrote

Richard Aldington in 1929. "Of course, no-body much bothered to read the lists. Why should they? The living must protect themselves from the dead, especially the intrusive dead. But the twentieth century had lost its Spring with a vengeance, so a good deal of forgetting had to be done."[21] The determination of "*had* to be done" suggests that, like Brittain, Aldington found remembering easier than forgetting.

It may be that the experience of the war would have best been forgotten, but it haunted the interwar years. In the writings of this period the war provides the substance of inspiration, even when it is not the subject.

NOTES

Preface

1. Mildred Aldrich, *When Johnny Comes Marching Home Again* (Boston: Small, Maynard and Co., 1919), 235.

2. *"Mademoiselle Miss": Letters from an American Girl Serving with the Rank of Lieutenant in a French Army Hospital at the Front* (Boston: W. A. Butterfield, 1916), 94.

3. Gertrude Stein, *The Autobiography of Alice B. Toklas* (1933; London: Penguin Books, 1966), 222.

4. Edith Wharton, *Fighting France* (New York: Charles Scribner's Sons, 1919), 177.

Chapter 1

1. Grey of Fallodon, *Twenty Five Years* (London: Hodder & Stoughton, 1926), 1:20.

2. See Paul Fussell, *The Great War and Modern Memory* (Oxford: Oxford University Press, 1975), chap. 2, "The Troglodyte World," which explains how

the experience of trench warfare changed our perception of landscape and the sky.

3. Laurence Binyon, "For the Fallen," *Poems of Our Time: 1900–1960* (London: Dent, 1963), 111. This quotation is still used at all remembrance services in Great Britain.

4. See Keith Robbins, *The First World War* (Oxford: Oxford University Press, 1984), 160–62, and Marc Ferro, *The Great War, 1914–1918* (London: Routledge & Kegan Paul, 1973), 170–71.

5. Grey, *Twenty Five Years*, 1:324. See also his speech before Parliament, 3 August 1914, app. 1.

6. Louis L. Snyder, *Historic Documents and World War I* (New York: Van Nostrand, 1958), 99.

7. Handbill quoted in Lyn Macdonald, *1914–1918: Voices and Images of the Great War* (London: Michael Joseph, 1988), 53.

8. Ibid., 69.

9. Quoted in Modris Eksteins, *Rites of Spring* (London: Black Swan, 1990), 201.

10. E. A. Mackintosh, "Recruiting," in *Up the Line to Death: The War Poets, 1914–1918,* ed. Brian Gardner (London: Methuen, 1964), 111–12.

11. Siegfried Sassoon, "Attack," in *Up the Line to Death,* 142.

12. Agnes Grozier Herbertson, "A Soldier's Face in a Starting Train," in *The Forgotten Army: Women's Poetry of the First World War,* ed. Nora Jones and Liz Ward (Beverly, Calif.: Highgate Publications, 1991), 8.

13. Valerie L. Esson, "The Scarlet Harvest," in *Forgotten Army,* 11.

14. Quoted in Anne Wiltsher, *Most Dangerous Women* (London: Pandora, 1985), 95.

15. Ibid., 101. Rosika Schwimmer was at the time of the Hague Conference International Press Secretary for International Women's Suffrage; Chrystal Macmillan, a leading British feminist, was a delegate at the conference and opposed the war; Jane Addams, founder of Chicago's Hull House settlement, was a highly respected American suffragist who also worked tirelessly to create new work opportunities for women; Aletta Jacobs was president of the Dutch Society for Women's Suffrage.

16. Wiltsher, *Most Dangerous Women,* 102.

17. Ibid., 6.

18. David Lloyd George, *War Memoirs* (London: Odhams, 1938), 1:211–31.

19. Ibid., 2:1247.

20. Quoted in Lyn Macdonald, *The Roses of No Man's Land* (London: Michael Joseph, 1980), 165. In what follows we are indebted to Lyn Macdonald, who performed an invaluable service in compiling this record of nursing experience and in depositing the originals in the Imperial War Museum.

21. Ibid., 190.

22. Ibid., 189.

23. Eksteins, *Rites of Spring,* 150.

24. Wilfred Owen, "Exposure," in *Up the Line to Death,* 137.

25. Gertrude Atherton predicted that such an armed rebellion would occur in her novel *The White Morning: A Novel of the Power of the German Women in Wartime* (New York: Frederick A. Stokes Co., 1918).

26. Quoted in Ferro, *The Great War*, 170.

27. See Arthur Marwick, *The Deluge: British Society and the First World War* (London: Macmillan, 1965), 89.

28. Lady Randolph Churchill, ed., *Women's War Work* (London: C. A. Pearson, 1916), 10.

29. Quoted by Deborah Thom in "Women and Work in Wartime Britain," in *The Upheaval of War,* ed. Richard Wall and Jay Winter (Cambridge: Cambridge University Press, 1988), 315.

30. See Lloyd George, *War Memoirs*, 1:175.

31. Quoted in Arthur Marwick, *Women at War, 1914–1918* (London: Fontana Paperbacks, 1977), 54.

32. Ibid., 87.

33. Letter to the editor, from "A Woman," *Morning Post*, 16 July 1915, quoted in *Behind the Lines: Gender and the Two World Wars*, ed. Margaret Randolph Higonnet, Jane Jenson, Sonya Michel, and Margaret Collins Weitz (New Haven and London: Yale University Press, 1987), 119.

34. Quoted in Marwick, *Women at War*, 91.

35. Thom, "Women and Work," 314.

36. Dorothy Littlejohn, unpublished manuscript, Imperial War Museum Archives (IWM).

37. D. E. Higgins, unpublished manuscript, IWM.

38. Macdonald, *Roses*, 165.

39. Ibid., 156.

40. Ibid., 186.

41. Ibid.

42. Ibid., 286.

43. Ibid., 291.

44. G. Holland, unpublished manuscript, IWM.

45. Sybil Harry, unpublished manuscript, IWM.

46. B. I. Rathbone, unpublished manuscript, IWM.

47. Marwick, *Women at War*, 68.

48. David Mitchell, *Women on the Warpath* (London: Jonathan Cape, 1965), 247–48.

49. Marwick, *Women at War*, 68.

50. Ibid.

51. Mrs. M. Brunskill Reid, unpublished manuscript, IWM.

52. B. I. Rathbone, unpublished manuscript, IWM.

Chapter 2

1. Brian Murdoch, "*Hinter Die Kulissen Des Krieges Sehen:* Adrienne Thomas, Evadne Price—and E. M. Remarke," *Forum for Modern Language Studies* 28, no. 1 (1992): 56.

2. Introduction, in *Behind the Lines*, 2.

3. John Silkin, "Introduction: A Prose Version of the First World War; Part One—The Writing of Britain and America," in *The Penguin Book of First World War Prose,* ed. Jon Glover and John Silkin (London: Penguin Books, 1990), 3.

4. Jean Bethke Elshtain, *Women and War* (Brighton: Harvester Press, 1987), 212, 213.

5. Ibid., 215.

6. Mildred Aldrich, *The Peak of the Load: The Waiting Months on the Hilltop from the Entrance of the Stars and Stripes to the Second Victory of the Marne* (Boston: Small, Maynard and Co., 1918), 117.

7. Elshtain, *Women and War*, 214.

8. Mildred Aldrich, *On the Edge of the War Zone: From the Battle of the Marne to the Entrance of the Stars and Stripes* (Boston: Small, Maynard and Co., 1917), 73–74, 75–76.

9. Janet Montefiore, " 'Shining Pins and Wailing Shells,' " in *Women and World War I: The Written Response,* ed. Dorothy Goldman (London: Macmillan, 1993), 64–65.

10. Barbara L. Baer, "Apart to the End?" *Commonweal,* 22 March 1985, 167.

11. Mary Roberts Rinehart, "Salvage," in *More Tish* (New York: A. L. Burt Co., 1921), 257.

12. See Willa Cather, *One of Ours* (New York: Alfred A. Knopf, 1923), 396–98, 445–54.

13. See Dorothy Canfield, "Vignettes from Life at the Rear," in *Home Fires in France* (New York: Henry Holt and Co., 1918), 70–74.

14. Claire M. Tylee, *The Great War and Women's Consciousness: Images of Militarism and Womanhood in Women's Writings, 1914–1964* (London: Macmillan, 1990), 182, 254.

15. Edith Wharton, *A Son at the Front* (New York: Charles Scribner's Sons, 1923), 190.

16. Ibid., 353.

17. Vera Brittain, *Testament of Youth* (London: Fontana/Virago, 1979), 195.

18. Aldrich, *On the Edge,* 21, 80–81, 296; *Peak of the Load,* 60, 105; and *When Johnny Comes Marching Home,* 81, 83.

19. Dorothy Canfield, "On the Edge," in *The Day of Glory* (New York: Henry Holt and Co., 1919), 3.

20. Ibid., 9–11.

21. Dorothy Canfield, "La Pharmacienne," in *Home Fires,* 285, 291. Retitled "Through Pity and Terror . . . " and reprinted in *A Harvest of Stories* (New York: Harcourt Brace and Co., 1956).

22. E. M. Delafield, *The War-Workers* (New York: Alfred A. Knopf, 1918), 278.

23. Mabel Potter Daggett, *Women Wanted: The Story Written in Blood Red Letters on the Horizon of the Great World War* (London: Hodder & Stoughton, 1918), 267.

24. See Dorothy Goldman, " 'Eagles of the West'? American Women Writers and World War I," in *Women and World War I.*

25. Elsie Janis, *The Big Show* (New York: Cosmopolitan Book Corporation, 1919), 19.

26. Wharton, *Fighting France,* 107.

27. Dorothy Canfield, "The Permissionnaire," in *Home Fires*, 54–55; retitled "In the Eye of the Storm" and reprinted in *Harvest of Stories*.

28. See, for example, the following accounts published anonymously: *A War Nurse's Diary* (New York: Macmillan, 1918), *Diary of a Nursing Sister on the Western Front* (London: William Blackwood, 1915), "*Mademoiselle Miss,*" and [Rebecca West], *War Nurse: The True Story of a Woman Who Lived, Loved, and Suffered on the Western Front* (New York: Cosmopolitan Book Corporation, 1930). Also see Enid Bagnold, *A Diary without Dates* (London: William Heinemann, 1918); Adele Bleneau, *The Nurse's Story in Which Reality Meets Romance* (Indianapolis: Bobbs-Merrill & Co., 1915); Mary Borden, *The Forbidden Zone* (London: Heinemann, 1929); Elsie Corbett, *Red Cross in Serbia 1915–1919: A Personal Diary of Experiences* (Banbury: Cheyney & Sons, 1964); Mabel Dearmer, *Letters from a Field Hospital* (Macmillan, 1926); Olive Dent, *A V.A.D. in France* (London: Grant Richards, 1917); Anne Donnell, *Letters of an Australian Army Sister* (1920); Florence Farmborough, *Nurse at the Russian Front: A Diary 1914–18* (London: Constable, 1974); R. E. Leake [Molly Skinner], *Letters of a V.A.D.* (London: Melrose, 1918); Mary Lee, "*It's a Great War!*" (Boston and New York: Houghton Mifflin Co., 1929); Sister K. E. Luard, *Unknown Warriors: Extracts from Letters of a Nursing Sister in France, 1914–1918* (London: Chatto & Windus, 1930); Mrs. Eva Shaw McLaren, *The History of the Scottish Women's Hospitals* (London: Hodder & Stoughton, 1919); Sister Martin-Nicholson, *My Experiences on Three Fronts* (London: George Allen and Unwin, n.d.); Nurse Shirley Millard, *I Saw Them Die* (London: Harrop, 1936); Flora Murray, *Women as Army Surgeons: Being the Story of the Women's Hospital Corps in Paris, Wimereux, and Endell Street: September 1914–October 1919* (London: Hodder & Stoughton, 1929); Violetta Thurstan, *Field Hospital and Flying Column: Being the Journal of an English Nursing Sister in Belgium and Russia* (London: Putnam's, 1915); Baroness T'Serclaes and Mairi Chisholm, *The Cellar-House of Pervyse: A Tale of Uncommon Things from the Journals and Letters of the Baroness T'Serclaes and Mairi Chisholm* (London: A. & C. Black, 1917); and Marie Van Vorst, *War Letters of an American Woman* (New York and London: John Lane Co., 1916).

29. Gertrude Atherton, *The Living Present* (New York: Frederick A. Stokes Co., 1917), 217.

30. Daggett, *Women Wanted*, 226–27.

31. Canfield, "On the Edge," 11.

32. Brittain, *Testament*, 164.

33. Harriet Stanton Blatch, *Mobilizing Women-Power* (New York: Woman's Press, 1916).

34. Mary Borden, "Blind," in *The Forbidden Zone* (London: Heinemann, 1929), 147.

35. Aldrich, *Peak of the Load*, 80.

36. Mrs. Humphry Ward, "*Missing*" (New York: Dodd, Mead and Co., 1918), 387.

37. Daggett, *Women Wanted*, 109.

38. Josephine Therese, *With Old Glory in Berlin* (Boston, Page Co., 1918), 70, 71. For other examples of women assuming the burden of men's work and

ensuring the survival of their community, see Mildred Aldrich, *A Hilltop on the Marne: Being Letters Written June 3–September 8, 1914* (Boston and New York: Houghton Mifflin Co., 1915), 69–71, and Gertrude Atherton, "The Silent Army," in *Living Present*, 24–34.

39. Nor is she alone: in this story the baker's wife and the mayor's wife also assume their husbands' responsibilities.

40. Atherton, *Living Present,* 39, 232.

41. Cather, *One of Ours,* 416.

42. Bessie Marchant, *A Girl Munition Worker* (London: Blackie and Son, n.d.), 132, 256.

43. T'Serclaes and Chisholm, *The Cellar-House of Pervyse,* 113–14. The episode is commemorated by a photograph. The two women were not unique; Eliott Paul records that Dr. Mary Walker "attended soldiers at the front and finally had her hair cut short and wore men's clothes, the latter by sanction of an act of Congress" (*Linden on the Saugus Branch* [New York: Random House, 1947], 273), and a similar ritual is described in the novel *"Not So Quiet . . ." Stepdaughters of War* (1930; London: Virago, 1988), 13–18, written by Evadne Price under the pseudonym Helen Zenna Smith, the name of the narrator.

44. Alice Cholmondeley [Elizabeth von Arnim], *Christine* (New York: Macmillan Co., 1917), introduction, n.p.

45. Daggett, *Women Wanted,* 110.

46. Wharton, *Fighting France,* 123; see also 61–66.

47. Dorothy Canfield, "France's Fighting Woman Doctor," in *Day of Glory,* 39.

48. Mary Agnes Hamilton, *Three against Fate: A Tale of 1917* (Cambridge, Mass.: Riverside Press, 1930), 131–32.

49. Antonia White, *Beyond the Glass* (1954); reprinted in *Frost in May* (London: Fontana, 1982), 428.

50. Wharton, *Son at the Front,* 123.

51. Canfield, "Vignettes," 61.

52. Meriel Buchanan, *Petrograd: The City of Trouble, 1914–1918* (London: W. Collins Sons & Co., 1918), 46.

53. Judith Sensibar, " 'Behind the Lines' in Edith Wharton's *A Son at the Front:* Rewriting a Masculinist Tradition," *Journal of American Studies* 24, no. 2 (1990): 188, 198.

54. For this brief analysis I am indebted to Jon Glover's "The Writing of Europe and Britain," in *Penguin Book of First World War Prose.*

55. Evadne Price did not herself serve abroad during the war. *"Not So Quiet"* does, however, contain much authentic detail about women's ambulance work on the western front taken from the unpublished diaries of a real ambulance driver, Winifred Young.

56. Murdoch, *"Hinter Die Kulissen,"* 60.

57. Ibid., 56, 74.

58. Helen Zenna Smith [Evadne Price], *Women of the Aftermath* (London: John Long, 1931), 120, 39.

59. May Sinclair, *The Tree of Heaven* (New York: Macmillan Co., 1917), 301.

60. Vera Brittain, unpublished letter, 19 February 1917, William Ready Division of Archives and Research Collections, McMaster University Library, Hamilton, Canada; hereafter cited as WRD. Quoted in Lynne Layton, "Vera Brittain's Testament(s)," in *Behind the Lines*, 73.

61. Rose Macaulay, *Told by an Idiot* (London: Constable, 1923), 141.

62. Temple Bailey, *The Tin Soldier* (New York: Grosset & Dunlap, 1918), 71.

63. Vera Brittain, unpublished letter, 14 October 1914, WRD. Quoted in Layton, "Vera Brittain's Testament(s)," 73.

64. Rinehart, "Salvage," 161.

65. Marchioness of Londonderry, *Retrospect* (London: Frederick Muller, 1938), 112.

66. Olive Dent, *A V.A.D. in France* (London: Grant Richards, 1917), 14–15.

67. Wharton, *Fighting France*, 62–63.

68. Helen Davenport Gibbons, *A Little Gray Home in France* (New York: Century Co., 1919), 153, 230. The modern tone of the last comment is reminiscent of Mabel Daggett's twice-repeated advice to women workers, " 'Don't darn' " (*Women Wanted*, 160, 184), or of the heroine's cri de coeur in Alice Cholmondeley's *Christine:* "She tends him as carefully as one would tend a baby, . . . and competently clears life round him all empty and free, so that he has room to work. I wish I had a wife" (87).

69. See, for example, Gertrude Atherton, *The White Morning;* Alice Cholmondeley, *Christine;* Mabel Daggett, *Women Wanted;* Christabel Pankhurst, writing in the *Suffragette;* and the Countess of Warwick, *A Woman and the War* (New York: George H. Doran, 1916).

70. Ward, "*Missing*," 395–96.

71. Atherton, *Living Present*, 208, 212, 272.

72. Daggett, *Women Wanted*, 269.

73. Murdoch, "*Hinter Die Kulissen*," 60.

74. Brittain, *Testament*, 401.

75. Ibid., 422.

76. Delafield, *War-Workers*, 10.

77. Ibid., 131.

78. Atherton, *White Morning*, 7–8.

79. Wharton, *Son at the Front*, 202, 222.

80. Elshtain, *Women and War*, 217.

81. Daggett, *Women Wanted,* 24, 170.

82. Sandra M. Gilbert, "Soldier's Heart: Literary Men, Literary Women, and the Great War," in *Behind the Lines*, 214, 200.

83. Atherton, *White Morning*, 2.

84. Ibid., 30.

85. Ibid., 64–65.

86. Ibid., 45, 94, 32–33.

87. Atherton, *Living Present*, 217, 218.

88. Margaret Higonnet and Patrice Higonnet, "The Double Helix," in *Behind the Lines*, 41–42.

89. Eksteins, *Rites of Spring*, 313.

90. Hamilton, *Three against Fate,* 81.

91. Eric J. Leed, *No Man's Land: Combat and Identity in World War I* (Cambridge: Cambridge University Press, 1979), 163.

92. Elaine Showalter, *The Female Malady: Women, Madness, and English Culture, 1830–1980* (London: Virago, 1987), 173.

93. Edith Wharton, *The Marne* (New York: D. Appleton and Co., 1918), 10.

94. Claire M. Tylee and Jane Marcus offer timely counterarguments to Gilbert. See, respectively, "Maleness Run Riot: The Great War and Women's Resistance to Militarism," *Women's Studies International Forum* 2, no. 3 (1988): 199–210, and "Corpus/Corps/Corpse: Writing the Body in/at War," in *Arms and the Women: War, Gender, and Literary Representation,* ed. Helen M. Cooper, Adrienne Auslander Munich, and Susan Merrill Squier (Chapel Hill and London: University of North Carolina Press, 1989), 124–67.

95. Tylee, *Great War and Women's Consciousness,* 55.

96. James Longenbach, "The Women and Men of 1914," in *Arms and the Women,* 104–5.

97. Brittain, *Testament,* 143, 215, 217.

98. Storm Jameson, *No Time Like the Present* (London: Caddell, 1933), 214.

99. Richard Aldington, *Death of a Hero* (London: Hogarth Press, 1929), 227.

100. Aldrich, *On the Edge,* 190, 192.

101. Gilbert, "Soldier's Heart," 199.

102. Rebecca West, *The Return of the Soldier* (Glasgow: Fontana/Virago, 1980), 20.

103. George Parfitt, *Fiction of the First World War: A Study* (London: Faber and Faber, 1988), 93.

104. West, *Return of the Soldier,* 111.

105. Virginia Woolf, *Mrs. Dalloway* (Harmondsworth: Penguin Books, 1972), 6–7.

106. Ibid., 62, 63, 64, 65, 64.

107. Ibid., 65.

108. Ibid., 66.

109. In *The Return of the Soldier,* just before Chris is brought back to the remembrance of who he is, Jenny comes across him sleeping while Margaret watches over him: "He lay there in the confident relaxation of a sleeping child, his hands unclenched and his head thrown back so that the bare throat showed defencelessly . . . [she had] gathered the soul of the man into her soul and is keeping it warm in love and peace. . . . That is a great thing for a woman to do" (86–87).

110. Gilbert, "Soldier's Heart," 212.

Chapter 3

1. See Fussell, *Great War,* and introduction, in *Penguin Book of First World War Prose.*

2. Fussell, *Great War*, 174

3. Virginia Woolf, "The Leaning Tower," in *Virginia Woolf: Collected Essays* (1940; London: Hogarth Press, 1960), 2:167.

4. Fussell, *Great War*, 115.

5. This is eloquently described by Fussell; see chaps. 2 and 4 of *The Great War*.

6. Fussell, *Great War*, 139.

7. Ibid., 136; George Orwell, "Boys' Weeklies," in *Critical Essays* (London: Secker and Warburg. 1954), 74.

8. Gillian Beer, *The Romance* (London: Methuen, 1986), 66.

9. See, for example, Bleneau's *The Nurse's Story in Which Reality Meets Romance* and [West's] *War Nurse: The True Story of a Woman Who Lived, Loved and Suffered on the Western Front*. One might argue that even that most idiosyncratic of forms, the war memoir, has romance configurations. Fussell suggests that "every successful memoir of that experience shares something with traditional literary romance" (*Great War*, 130). In *Dangerous by Degrees: Women at Oxford and the Somerville College Novelists* (New Brunswick: Rutgers University Press, 1989), 222, Susan J. Leonardi notes that Brittain's *Testament of Youth* is built on the structure of romantic comedy, ending as it does, after years of grief and isolation, in the traditional comic conclusion of marriage.

10. Review of May Sinclair's *A Journal of Impressions in Belgium*, *Times Literary Supplement*, 26 August 1915, 282.

11. Frederic Jameson, "Magical Narratives: Romance as Genre," *New Literary History* 7 (1975): 158.

12. Sandra Gilbert and Susan Gubar, *The Madwoman in the Attic: The Woman Writer and the Nineteenth-Century Literary Imagination* (New Haven: Yale University Press, 1979).

13. Rachel Blau DuPlessis, *Writing Beyond the Ending: Narrative Strategies of Twentieth-Century Women Writers* (Bloomington: Indiana University Press, 1985), 5.

14. *Times History of the War* (London: Times, 1915), 4:245.

15. Fussell, *Great War*, 155.

16. Katherine Mansfield, 10 November 1919, *Letters and Journals of Katherine Mansfield: A Selection*, ed. C. K. Stead (Harmondsworth: Penguin, 1977), 147.

17. Dorothy Stanley, *Miss Pim's Camouflage* (London: Hutchinson, 1918), 53

18. Ibid., 124, 222.

19. Ibid., 168.

20. See Frederic Jameson, "Modernism and Imperialism," in *Nationalism, Colonialism, and Literature*, ed. Terry Eagleton (Minneapolis: University of Minnesota Press, 1990), 49, for an account of the ways in which Germans had been regarded as "quintessential ogres and bogeymen of childhood nightmare, physically alien and terrifying, barbarous, uncivilised."

21. Orwell, "Boys' Weeklies," 74.

22. Review of Dorothy Stanley's *Miss Pim's Camouflage*, *Times Literary Supplement*, 9 May 1918, 220.

23. Stanley, *Miss Pim's Camouflage,* 5–6, 9.

24. Northrop Frye, *Anatomy of Criticism: Four Essays* (Princeton, N.J.: Princeton University Press, 1957), 193.

25. Stanley, *Miss Pim's Camouflage,* 256.

26. Cicely Hamilton, *William—An Englishman* (London: Skeffington and Son, 1919), 57–58.

27. Ibid., 138.

28. Ibid., 218.

29. Ibid., 179, 222, 238, 250.

30. Review of Cicely Hamilton's *William—An Englishman, Times Literary Supplement,* 27 February 1919, 111.

31. Hamilton, *William—An Englishman,* 223.

32. Nicola Beauman, *A Very Great Profession: The Woman's Novel, 1914–39* (London: Virago Press, 1983), 28.

33. Philip Hager, *The Novels of World War I—An Annotated Bibliography* (New York: Garland, 1981), 123, and Tylee, *Great War and Women's Consciousness,* 139.

34. Cicely Hamilton, *Life Errant* (London: Dent, 1935), 84.

35. May Sinclair, *The Romantic* (London: Collins, 1920), 67, 29–30.

36. Tylee, *Great War and Women's Consciousness,* 125.

37. Sinclair, *The Romantic,* 59. How women writers were able to employ a confident tone ("she knew") to express uncertainty ("She wondered whether any of them really knew") is discussed further in chap. 4.

38. Sinclair, *The Romantic,* 190.

39. Ibid., 174–75.

40. Ibid., 237.

41. Ibid., 69.

42. Ibid., 244, 245, 247.

43. See Gilbert, "Soldier's Heart."

44. Enid Bagnold, *The Happy Foreigner* (London: Virago, 1987), publisher's description.

45. Enid Bagnold, *The Happy Foreigner* (1920; London: Heinemann, 1929), 65, 34; all references are to this edition.

46. Katherine Mansfield, review of *The Happy Foreigner* reprinted in *Novels and Novelists,* ed. J. Middleton Murry (London: Constable, 1930), 224.

47. Bagnold, *Happy Foreigner,* 275.

48. Ibid., 288.

49. Ibid., 291; Bagnold dwelt on the importance of her writing: "Even at a kiss there was a comment more valuable than the kiss. I was the recording Angel and that was my protection and my armour. I am not a born writer, but I was born a writer. Everything would serve." From *Enid Bagnold's Autobiography* (1889; London: Heinemann, 1969), 107.

50. Gilbert, "Soldier's Heart," 200.

51. The discussion that follows excludes Stanley's *Miss Pim's Camouflage,* which is notably not a feminist text.

52. Canfield, "La Pharmacienne," 313.

53. West, *Return of the Soldier,* 21.

54. Marwick, *The Deluge,* 278.

55. *The Diary of Virginia Woolf: Volume I, 1915–19*, ed. Anne Olivier Bell (Harmondsworth: Penguin Books, 1977), 217–18.

56. Jameson, "Modernism and Imperialism," 158.

57. [West], *War Nurse*, 45, 263, 154–55.

58. Ibid., 157.

59. Erich Maria Remarque, *All Quiet on the Western Front*, trans. A. H. Wheen (1928; London: Pan, 1987), epigraph.

60. Smith [Price], *"Not So Quiet,"* 94, 55.

61. Ibid., 217.

62. Review of *The Happy Foreigner, Times Literary Supplement*, 1 July 1920, 422.

63. Barbara Hardy, introduction, in *"Not So Quiet,"* 12.

64. H. M. Tomlinson, "War Books," *Criterion* 36 (1930): 404.

65. Jameson, "Modernism and Imperialism," 146.

66. Katherine Mansfield, "An Indiscreet Journey," in *The Stories of Katherine Mansfield*, ed. Anthony Alpers (Oxford: Oxford University Press, 1984), 181.

67. Mansfield, "An Indiscreet Journey," 185, 186.

68. Claire Tylee points out that the tale should not be read as simply narrating a sexual adventure; the story, however, also exceeds other social interpretations, including the one Tylee proffers—that it concerns the "squalid, profane reality of the war-zone" (Tylee, *Great War and Women's Consciousness*, 89).

69. For further discussion of this phenomenon, see chap. 5.

70. In chap. 4 of *The Great War*, Fussell describes the way that accounts of combat made use of the genre. Popular war romances written by men include, for example, Burton Stevenson's *Little Comrade: A Tale of the Great War* (New York, Henry Holt and Co., 1915).

71. See Tylee, *Great War and Women's Consciousness*, 93–94.

72. Radclyffe Hall, "Miss Ogilvy Finds Herself," in *Miss Ogilvy Finds Herself* (1926; London: Hammond, Hammond, 1934).

73. Ibid., 10, 18.

Chapter 4

1. Parfitt, *Fiction of the First World War*, 6.

2. Ward, *"Missing,"* 195.

3. Mary Borden, "Moonlight," in *Forbidden Zone*, 52, 57, 60–61. Although not published until 1929, the book was written during the war.

4. Beatrice Harraden, *Where Your Treasure Is* (London: Hutchinson, 1918), 80.

5. Brittain, *Testament*, 133.

6. Aldrich, *On the Edge*, 103.

7. Ward, *"Missing,"* 55.

8. Ibid., 55–56.

9. Fussell, *Great War*, 57.

10. Sylvia Thompson, *The Hounds of Spring* (New York: Grosset and Dunlap, 1926), 225, 246.

11. James Longenbach argues that "the Great War was not the first military conflict in which British women played a prominent part, and the women of 1914

had several role models" (see "The Women and Men of 1914," 101). Although he instances the influential chapter "Women and War" in Olive Schreiner's *Women and Labour* (London, 1911) and Mrs. St. Clair Stobart's *War and Women* (London, 1913), two books hardly constitute a supportive tradition on which women writers could draw—and especially not in the writing of fiction.

12. Bernard Bergonzi, *Heroes' Twilight: A Study of the Literature of the Great War* (London: Constable and Co., 1965), 41.

13. Brittain, *Testament*, 417.

14. Borden, preface, in *Forbidden Zone*, n.p.

15. The reliance on combat as a definitional criterion is found in women critics as much as in men. Gilbert writes that "From the first . . . World War I fostered characteristically modernist irony in *young men,* inducting them into 'death's dream kingdom' by revealing exactly how spurious were their visions of heroism" (emphasis added; see "Soldier's Heart," 201). Or consider this from Elshtain: "*male* modernists offer the critical distancing from war and the reflective puncturing of war myths that most powerfully served to defeat the simplistic, hollow heroics characterizing the Western World's plunge into the First World War." How easy it is to allow this apparently plausible line of thought to contribute to unjust conclusions is apparent in Elshtain's criticism of Cather's *One of Ours* for its "literary reinscription of . . . jubilant innocence as the war dragged to its bitter end, plummeting from all the high hopes that had marked its beginning, illusions from which Europeans had become rapidly disenchanted—*or at least those fighting the war had.* Wholly without irony, Cather's prose grates. Its apotheosis of war is sicklied with an abstract sense of sentimentalism" (emphasis added; see *Women and War,* 217).

16. Eksteins, *Rites of Spring,* 296. Elshtain makes an implicit contrast between women and men writers when she says that "Unlike Cather, who unselfconsciously uses words of sacrifice, honor, ecstasy, freedom, Hemingway enunciates what became the modernist understanding—bitter, ironic" (*Women and War,* 218).

17. Roland Dorgeles, *Souvenirs sur les Croix de bois* (Paris, 1929), 10, quoted in Eksteins, *Rites of Spring,* 295–96.

18. Ernest Hemingway, *A Farewell to Arms* (New York: Charles Scribner's Sons, 1929), 191.

19. Catherine Reilly, introduction, in *Scars upon My Heart: Women's Poetry and Verse of the First World War (London: Virago, 1981),* xxxv.

20. Elshtain, *Women and War,* 165.

21. Bailey, *Tin Soldier,* 96.

22. Borden, "The Regiment," in *Forbidden Zone,* 21, 23.

23. Herbert Read, *Art Now* (London: Faber and Faber, 1933).

24. Richard Aldington, "In the Tube," *Egoist,* 1 May 1915, 74.

25. After H. D.'s poem in the 1 May 1915 *Egoist* there appears (on p. 75) the first printed version of D. H. Lawrence's "Eloi, Eloi, Lama Sabachthani?"

> Why should we hate, then, with this hate incarnate?
> Why am I a bridegroom of War, war's paramour?
> What is the crime, that my seed is turned to blood,
> My kiss to wounds?

My kiss to wounds?
Who is it will have it so, who did the crime?
And why do the women follow us satisfied,
Feed on our wounds like bread, receive our blood
Like glittering seed upon them for fulfilment?

This complex poem unleashes the pent-up energy of combat, seen in terms of sexual conflict expressed through a homosexual crucifixion. Lawrence gives voice to the deep anxieties the war produced, just as in his early fiction the war was closely associated with complex relationships between men and women.

26. Malcolm Bradbury, "The Denuded Place: War and Form in *Parade's End* and *USA*," in *The First World War in Fiction*, ed. Holger Klein (London: Macmillan, 1976), 193–94.

27. Eksteins, *Rites of Spring*, 285.

28. See Longenbach, "The Women and Men of 1914," 97–123.

29. Sinclair, *Tree of Heaven*, 233, 162.

30. Ibid., 199, 163.

31. Borden, "The Captive Balloon," in *Forbidden Zone*, 13, 14.

32. "The Captive Balloon" extends incomprehension almost into surrealism. Its subject is described as "an oyster in the sky keeping an eye on the Germans" (*Forbidden Zone*, 12).

33. Borden, "The City in the Desert," in *Forbidden Zone*, 111, 113.

34. Ibid., 113.

35. Eksteins, *Rites of Spring*, 287.

36. Parfitt, *Fiction of the First World War*, 5–6. Robert Graves, writing about the structure of *Good-bye to All That*, explains that the book was "roughly organized in my mind in the form of a number of short stories, which is the way that people find it easier to be interested in. . . . They like what they call 'situations' " ("P.S. Good-bye to All That," in *But It Still Goes On* [London: Cape, 1930], 6; quoted in Fussell, *Great War*, 205).

37. Parfitt, *Fiction of the First World War*, 48–49.

38. Canfield, publisher's note, in *Home Fires*, n.p. It is so apposite that one wonders if Canfield wrote it herself.

39. Canfield, "Permissionnaire," in *Home Fires*, 27.

40. Ibid., 33, 35.

41. Canfield, "Notes from a French Village in the War Zone," in *Home Fires*, 6, 7, 9. For similar references see, for example, 98, 261, 265.

42. Similarly, Canfield's *The Day of Glory* contains "Some Confused Impressions." This strategy is also echoed by women writers with no literary pretensions: Olive Dent's *A V.A.D in France*, which describes nursing under canvas, is made up of fragments: articles, selections from a diary, a chapter entirely in dialogue, letters, and menus.

43. Elshtain, *Women and War*, xii.

44. Borden, preface, in *Forbidden Zone*, n.p.

45. Borden, "City in the Desert," in *Forbidden Zone*, 111, 113, 114.

46. Borden, "Conspiracy," in *Forbidden Zone*, 118, 119–20.

47. Borden, "Paraphernalia," in *Forbidden Zone*, 124.

48. Tylee, *Great War and Women's Consciousness*, 97.

49. Ellen La Motte, *Backwash of War* (1916; London: Puttnam, 1934), 83–84.

50. Glover, "Writing of Europe and Britain," 11.

51. Borden, "Moonlight," in *Forbidden Zone*, 59, 60.

52. Hamilton, *Three against Fate*, 21.

53. Frederick J. Hoffman, *The Twenties* (1949; New York: Collier, 1962), 57.

54. Tylee, *Great War and Women's Consciousness*, 114.

55. Rose Macaulay, *Non-Combatants and Others* (1916; London: Methuen, 1986), 129. Compare the title of Canfield's "On the Edge."

56. Eksteins, *Rites of Spring*, 343–44.

57. Women have, after all, clear claim to this territory: it was May Sinclair who coined the phrase "stream of consciousness" in a review of the novels of Dorothy Richardson (*Egoist,* April 1918). See also Virginia Woolf's musings on the idea of a "woman's sentence" as providing an alternative to the realist style of men novelists.

58. Hamilton, *Three against Fate*, 238.

59. Virginia Woolf, *Jacob's Room* (1922; London: Hogarth Press, 1949), 175.

60. West, *Return of the Soldier*, 98, 99.

61. Woolf, *Mrs. Dalloway*, 18, 206.

62. Ibid., 134, 135.

63. Claire Tylee suggests that Cicely Hamilton's novel *William—An Englishman* can be understood by conflating the hero and heroine into one: the novel "is a myth about what Cicely Hamilton had called 'the battle of life' for the independent woman at the time of the First World War. William and Griselda are male and female counterparts, whose 'two hearts beat as one,' the masculine and feminine aspects of a single, female self" (Tylee, *Great War and Women's Consciousness,* 140). This topic is discussed at greater length in chap. 3.

64. Daggett, *Women Wanted*, 110, 12.

65. Aldrich, *Hilltop on the Marne*, 173.

66. Borden, "Conspiracy," in *Forbidden Zone*, 117.

67. Radclyffe Hall, "Fräulein Schwartz," in *Miss Ogilvy*, 132.

68. The reverse of the story can be found in Alice Cholmondeley's *Christine;* there, the English heroine, studying music in Berlin, writes to her mother that the other boarders "all fix their eyes reproachfully on me while as one man they tell me how awful my country is. Do people in London boarding houses tell the German boarders how awful Germany is, I wonder? I don't believe they do" (28).

69. Introduction, in *Behind the Lines*, 15.

70. Radclyffe Hall, *The Well of Loneliness* (London: Cape, 1928), 306, 311.

71. Hall, "Miss Ogilvy," 13, 14, 22.

72. Although some of the issues about women's wearing uniforms illustrated in chap. 1 may have concealed fears of lesbianism, the more common worry concerned the possible breakdown of the relationship between the sexes, outlined in chap. 2. The two can be found in a conflated form, as in Gertrude Atherton's *The White Morning*, whose heroine, Gisela Niebuhr, rejects heterosexual love. The sexual attraction she feels for Franz Nettelbeck only makes her

"angry and humiliated in her surrender and secret chaos," and eventually she murders him. Romance is replaced by her feelings for women: she experiences "a sudden inclusive love of her sex, an overpowering desire to deliver it from the sadness and horror of war . . . she gave her real sympathies and affections to her women friends" (27, 67, 68).

73. Pamela Hinkson, *The Ladies' Road* (London: Gollancz, 1932), 217, 313.
74. Gilbert, "Soldier's Heart," 200.
75. Borden, "The Square," in *Forbidden Zone*, 15, 16.
76. Muriel Spark, "The First Year of My Life," in *The Stories of Muriel Spark* (London: Bodley Head, 1985), 265, 267, 256, 268.
77. Hamilton, *Three against Fate*, 149–50.
78. Ibid., 151, 158.
79. Tylee, *Great War and Women's Consciousness*, 187.
80. Parfitt, *Fiction of the First World War*, 43.
81. Glover, "Writing of Europe and Britain," 11.
82. Ibid., 11–12.
83. Parfitt, *Fiction of the First World War*, 4–5.
84. Introduction, in *Behind the Lines*, 7.

Chapter 5

1. An up-to-date bibliography (primary and secondary sources) of women's writing about the war would be a welcome tool for scholars and go some way toward redressing earlier neglect.
2. Gilbert, "Soldier's Heart," 222.
3. Brittain, *Testament*, 251–52.
4. Ibid., 145, 151.
5. Ibid., 145.
6. H. D., "Thorn Thicket," unpublished manuscript held at the Beinecke Library, Yale University, New Haven, Conn.; quoted in Gilbert, "Soldier's Heart," 222.
7. Ibid., 222–23.
8. Wharton, *Son at the Front*, 95, 128.
9. Sharon Ouditt, *Fighting Forces, Writing Women: Identity and Ideology of the First World War* (London and New York: Routledge, 1994), 31.
10. Stein, *Autobiography of Alice B. Toklas*, 201.
11. Ibid., 203.
12. Atherton, *Living Present*, 126–27.
13. Aldrich, *On the Edge*, 14.
14. Ibid., 144, 146, 136, 148.
15. Aldrich, *Peak of the Load*, 25.
16. Ibid., 40.
17. Eksteins, *Rites of Spring*, 238.
18. Daggett, *Women Wanted*, 40.
19. Judith Kazantzis, preface, in *Scars upon My Heart*, xix.
20. Dent, *V.A.D in France*, 219–20.
21. Kazantzis, preface, in *Scars upon My Heart*, xxiii.
22. Tylee, *Great War and Women's Consciousness*, 188.

23. Ibid., 256.

24. Flora Sandes, *An English Woman-Sergeant in the Serbian Army* (London, New York, Toronto: Hodder and Stoughton, 1916), 36–37.

25. Tylee, *Great War and Women's Consciousness*, 141, 142.

26. Dent, *V.A.D in France*, 227–28.

27. It is interesting to find this expression of women's understanding of their exclusion from official history—which has more recently been a cornerstone of women's studies—identified as early as 1917, and by a writer who would lay no claim to radical insight or attitude.

28. Eksteins, *Rites of Spring*, 17.

29. Aldrich, *On the Edge*, 1.

30. Ibid., 64. For a further example of the importance Aldrich allots to paper and papers, see letter 15 of *On the Edge* and the interlinking commentary in her short-story collection *Told in a French Garden* (Boston: Small, Maynard & Co., 1916).

31. Aldrich, *On the Edge*, 64.

32. Canfield, "Some Confused Impressions," in *Day of Glory*, 109, 111.

33. Ibid., 111.

34. Introduction, in *Behind the Lines*, 14.

35. Peter Aichinger, *The American Soldier in Fiction* (Ames: Iowa State University Press, 1975), 4.

36. One almost expects him to suggest that they should not puzzle their pretty little heads about it.

37. Macaulay, *Non-Combatants and Others*, 21.

38. Hinkson, *The Ladies' Road*, 186.

39. Brittain, *Testament*, 45, 176, 339, 475, 496.

40. Borden, preface, in *Forbidden Zone*, n.p.

41. Ouditt, *Fighting Forces, Writing Women*, 36.

42. Ruth S. Farnam, *A Nation at Bay* (Indianapolis: Bobbs-Merrill Co., 1918), 16–18.

43. Wharton, *Son at the Front*, 375.

44. Sandes, *English Woman-Sergeant*, 161–62.

45. Kazantzis, preface, in *Scars upon My Heart*, xxiii–xxiv.

46. Cather, *One of Ours*, 391; Hamilton, *Three against Fate*, 81; Alice B. Emerson, *Ruth Fielding in the Red Cross* (New York: Cupples & Leon Co., 1918), 132.

47. Wharton, *The Marne*, 61–62, 97–98.

48. Aldrich, *Hilltop on the Marne*, 58–59.

49. Aldrich, *Peak of the Load*, 61.

50. Brittain, *Testament*, 45, 51.

51. Aldrich, *On the Edge*, 176–77.

52. Brittain, *Testament*, 387.

53. Sandes, *English Woman-Sergeant*, 30, 38.

54. Mrs. Humphry Ward, *Towards the Goal* (London: John Murray, 1917), 244.

55. Brittain, *Testament*, 291.

56. Eksteins, *Rites of Spring*, 246.

57. Aldrich, *On the Edge*, 43, 105.

58. Rinehart, "Tish Does Her Bit," in *More Tish*, 138–39 (the story was first published in 1917).

59. Brittain, *Testament*, 423.

60. Elshtain, *Women and War*, 248.

61. Dent, *V.A.D in France*, 14–15.

62. Smith [Price], *"Not So Quiet,"* 239.

63. Virginia Woolf, *A Writer's Diary*, ed. Leonard Woolf (New York: Harcourt Brace and Co., 1954), 101, 103, 98, 87.

64. Virginia Woolf, *To the Lighthouse* (New York: Harcourt, Brace & Co., 1927), 196.

65. Ibid., 192, 194, 198, 199, 202.

66. Of a similarly bracketed passage in *Orlando* (1928), which deals with celebrations at the conclusion of the hero/heroine's law case, Woolf writes, "all of which is properly enclosed in square brackets . . . for the good reasons that a parenthesis it was without importance in Orlando's life" (Virginia Woolf, *Orlando* [New York: Signet Books, 1960], 167).

67. Woolf, *To the Lighthouse,* 191, 193, 198, 199.

68. Ibid., 200, 202.

69. A similar contrast occurs in *Orlando* when the hero/heroine considers with her maid how to maintain the fabric of her house. The latter blames the Prince Consort for a hole in a sheet: " 'Sale bosch!' she said (for there had been another war; this time against the Germans). 'Sheets for a double bed,' Orlando repeated dreamily" (197).

70. Ouditt, *Fighting Forces, Writing Women*, 176.

71. Woolf, *To the Lighthouse*, 202.

72. Joan W. Scott, "Rewriting History," in *Behind the Lines*, 28. Sandra Gilbert, writing of "the apocalyptic events of this war," suggests that "the Great War . . . is one of those classic cases of dissonance between the official, male-centred history and unofficial female history" ("Soldier's Heart," 199).

73. Introduction, in *Behind the Lines*, 7.

74. Helen Thomas, *As It Was . . . World without End* (London: Heinemann, 1935), 311–12.

75. Edward Thomas, "War Diary," in *Penguin Book of First World War Prose*, 54.

Chapter 6

1. Aldrich, *Peak of the Load*, 106.

2. Bailey, *Tin Soldier*, 174.

3. Atherton, *Living Present*, 212–13, 271–72.

4. Daggett, *Women Wanted*, 59.

5. Atherton, *Living Present*, 207–8.

6. Ibid., 206–7, 213.

7. Ibid., 238.

8. Ibid., 212–13, 194.

9. Scott, "Rewriting History," 27.

10. Brittain, *Testament*, 504.

11. Ibid., 73, 404.

12. Ibid., 27, 490.
13. Ibid., 490.
14. Ibid., 622.
15. Eksteins, *Rites of Spring,* 376.
16. Vera Brittain, *Dark Tide* (1923; New York: Macmillan, 1936), 204.
17. Brittain, *Testament,* 580, 651–52.
18. Ibid., 655.
19. Alison Light, *Forever England: Femininity, Literature, and Conservatism between the Wars* (London: Routledge, 1991), 210.
20. Lee, *"It's a Great War!"* 575.
21. Aldington, *Death of a Hero,* 11.

SELECTED BIBLIOGRAPHY

The following bibliography is divided into primary sources, including fiction, nonfiction, and anthologies, and secondary sources, the latter being divided between books that deal with the history of the war and its cultural impact, including bibliographies, and books of literary criticism. Commentary on women's roles and writing in the Great War has characteristically been marked by a cross-disciplinary approach—historical, literary, political, cultural—and we acknowledge that the distinction between the categories below is not as clear cut as it might be.

PRIMARY SOURCES

Aldrich, Mildred. *A Hilltop on the Marne: Being Letters Written June 3–September 8, 1914.* Boston and New York: Houghton Mifflin Co., 1915.
———. *On the Edge of the War Zone: From the Battle of the Marne to the Entrance of the Stars and Stripes.* Boston: Small, Maynard and Co., 1917.

————. *The Peak of the Load: The Waiting Months on the Hilltop from the Entrance of the Stars and Stripes to the Second Victory of the Marne*. Boston: Small, Maynard and Co., 1918.

————. *When Johnny Comes Marching Home*. Boston: Small, Maynard and Co., 1919.

Atherton, Gertrude. *The Living Present*. New York: Frederick A. Stokes Co., 1917.

————. *The White Morning: A Novel of the Power of the German Women in Wartime*. New York: Frederick A. Stokes Co., 1918.

Bagnold, Enid. *A Diary without Dates*. London: William Heinemann, 1918.

————. *The Happy Foreigner*. 1920. London: William Heinemann, 1929.

Borden, Mary. *The Forbidden Zone*. London: William Heinemann, 1929.

Brittain, Vera. *Testament of Youth*. 1933. Reprint. London: Fontana/Virago, 1979.

————. *War Diary, 1913–1917: Chronicle of Youth*. Edited by Alan Bishop, with Terry Smart. London: Victor Gollancz, 1981.

Canfield, Dorothy. *The Day of Glory*. New York: Henry Holt and Co., 1919.

————. *Home Fires in France*. New York: Henry Holt and Co., 1918.

Cather, Willa. *One of Ours*. New York: Alfred A. Knopf, 1923.

Cholmondeley, Alice [Elizabeth von Arnim]. *Christine*. New York: Macmillan, 1917.

Daggett, Mabel Potter. *Women Wanted: The Story Written in Blood Red Letters on the Horizon of the Great World War*. London: Hodder & Stoughton, 1918.

Delafield, E. M. [Esmée de la Pasture]. *The War-Workers*. London: William Heinemann, 1918.

Dent, Olive. *A V.A.D. in France*. London: Grant Richards, 1917.

Farmborough, Florence. *Nurse at the Russian Front: A Diary 1914–18*. London: Constable, 1974.

Glover, Jon, and John Silkin, eds. *The Penguin Book of First World War Prose*. London: Penguin Books, 1990.

Hall, Radclyffe. *Miss Ogilvy Finds Herself*. 1934. Reprint. London: Hammond, Hammond, 1959.

————. *The Well of Loneliness*. London: Cape, 1928.

Hamilton, Cicely. *Life Errant*. London: Dent, 1935.

————. *William—An Englishman*. London: Skeffington and Son, 1919.

Hamilton, Mary Agnes. *Three against Fate*. Cambridge, Mass.: Riverside Press, 1930.

H. D. [Hilda Doolittle]. *Bid Me to Live: A Madrigal*. 1960. Reprint. London: Virago Press, 1984.

Hinkson, Pamela. *The Ladies' Road*. London: Gollancz, 1932.

Jameson, Storm. *No Time Like the Present*. London: Caddell, 1933.

Lee, Mary. *"It's a Great War!"* Boston and New York: Houghton Mifflin Co., 1929.

Macaulay, Rose. *Non-Combatants and Others*. 1916. Reprint. London: Methuen, 1986.

————. *Told by an Idiot*. London: Constable, 1923.

Mansfield, Katherine. "An Indiscreet Journey." In *Something Childish and Other Stories*. 1924. Reprinted in *The Stories of Katherine Mansfield*, edited by A. Alpers, 628–44. Oxford: Oxford University Press, 1984.

————. *Letters and Journals of Katherine Mansfield: A Selection.* Edited by C. K. Stead. Harmondsworth: Penguin, 1977.

Rathbone, Irene. *We That Were Young.* 1932. Reprint. London: Virago, 1988.

Reilly, Catherine, ed. *Scars upon My Heart: Women's Poetry and Verse of the First World War.* London: Virago, 1981.

Remarque, Erich Maria. *All Quiet on the Western Front.* 1929. Reprint. London: Mayflower Books, 1963.

Rinehart, Mary Roberts. "Salvage." In *More Tish.* New York: A. L. Burt Co., 1921.

Sandes, Flora. *An English Woman-Sergeant in the Serbian Army.* London: Hodder and Stoughton, 1916.

Sinclair, May. *A Journal of Impressions in Belgium.* London: Hutchinson, 1915.

————. *The Romantic.* London: W. Collins, 1920.

————. *The Tree of Heaven.* London: Cassell, 1917.

Smith, Helen Zenna [Evadne Price]. *"Not So Quiet . . ." Stepdaughters of War.* 1930. London: Virago, 1988.

————. *Women of the Aftermath.* London: John Long, 1931.

Stanley, Dorothy. *Miss Pim's Camouflage.* London: Hutchinson, 1918.

Stein, Gertrude. *The Autobiography of Alice B. Toklas.* 1933. Reprint. London: Penguin Books, 1966.

Thomas, Helen. *"As It Was" and "World without End."* 1926, 1931. London: William Heinemann, 1935.

Thompson, Sylvia. *The Hounds of Spring.* London: William Heinemann, 1926.

Thurstan, Violetta. *Field Hospital and Flying Column: Being the Journal of an English Nursing Sister in Belgium and Russia.* London: Puttnam, 1915.

T'Serclaes, Baroness, and Mairi Chisholm. *The Cellar-House of Pervyse: A Tale of Uncommon Things from the Journals and Letters of the Baroness T'Serclaes and Mairi Chisholm.* London: A. & C. Black, 1917.

Ward, Mrs. Humphry. *"Missing."* New York: Dodd, Mead and Co., 1918.

————. *Towards the Goal: Letters on Great Britain's Behalf in the War.* London: John Murray, 1917.

West, Rebecca. *The Return of the Soldier.* 1918. Glasgow: Fontana/Virago, 1980.

[West, Rebecca.] *War Nurse: The True Story of a Woman Who Lived, Loved, and Suffered on the Western Front.* New York: Cosmopolitan Book Corp., 1930.

Wharton, Edith. *Fighting France.* New York: Charles Scribner's Sons, 1919.

————. *The Marne: A Story of the War.* New York: D. Appleton and Co., 1918.

————. *A Son at the Front.* New York: Charles Scribner's Sons, 1923.

White, Antonia. *Beyond the Glass.* 1954. Reprinted in *Frost in May.* London: Fontana, 1982.

Woolf, Virginia. *The Diary, Volume 1: 1915–1919.* Edited by Anne Olivier Bell. London: Penguin Books, 1977.

————. *Jacob's Room.* London: Hogarth Press, 1922.

————. *Mrs. Dalloway.* 1925. Harmondsworth: Penguin Books, 1972.

————. *Three Guineas.* London: Hogarth Press, 1938.

————. *To the Lighthouse.* London: Hogarth Press, 1927.

SECONDARY SOURCES

History of the War and Its Cultural Impact

Baer, Barbara L. "Apart to the End?" *Commonweal*, 22 March 1985.

Braybon, Gail. *Women Workers in the First World War: The British Experience*. London: Croom Helm, 1981.

Buitenhuis, Peter. *The Great War of Words: Literature as Propaganda, 1914–18 and After*. London: Batsford, 1989.

Byles, Joan Montgomery. "Women's Experience of World War I: Suffragists, Pacifists, and Poets." *Women's Studies International Forum* 8, no. 5 (1985).

Condell, Diana, and Jean Liddiard. *Working for Victory? Images of Women in the First World War*. London: Routledge, 1987.

Dangerfield, George. *The Strange Death of Liberal England*. London: Constable, 1935.

Eksteins, Modris. *Rites of Spring: The Great War and the Birth of the Modern Age*. London: Black Swan, 1990.

Elshtain, Jean Bethke. *Women and War*. Brighton: Harvester Press, 1987.

Falls, Cyril. *War Books: A Critical Guide*. London: Davies, 1930.

Ferro, Marc. *The Great War, 1914–1918*. London: Routledge & Kegan Paul, 1973.

George, David Lloyd. *War Memoirs*. 2 vols. London: Odhams, 1938.

Greenwald, Maurine. *Women, War, and Work: The Impact of World War I on Women Workers in the United States*. Westport, Conn.: Greenwood Press, 1980.

Grey of Fallodon, *Twenty Five Years*. 2 vols. London: Hodder & Stoughton, 1926.

Hager, Philip E., and D. Taylor. *The Novels of World War I: An Annotated Bibliography*. New York: Garland, 1982.

Higonnet, Margaret Randolph, Jane Jenson, Sonya Michel, and Margaret Collins Weitz, eds. *Behind the Lines: Gender and the Two World Wars*. New Haven and London: Yale University Press, 1987.

Leed, Eric J. *No Man's Land: Combat and Identity in World War I*. Cambridge: Cambridge University Press, 1979.

Macdonald, Lyn. *1914–1918: Voices and Images of the Great War*. London: Michael Joseph, 1988.

———. *The Roses of No Man's Land*. London: Michael Joseph, 1980.

Marwick, Arthur. *The Deluge: British Society and the First World War*. London: Macmillan, 1965.

———. *Women at War, 1914–1918*. London: Fontana Paperbacks, 1977.

Mitchell, David. *Monstrous Regiment: The Story of the Women of the First World War*. New York: Macmillan Co., 1965.

———. *Women on the Warpath: The Story of the Women of the First World War*. London: Jonathan Cape, 1965.

Robbins, Keith. *The First World War*. Oxford: Oxford University Press, 1984.

Taylor, A. J. P. *English History, 1914–1945*. Oxford: Clarendon Press, 1965.

———. *The First World War*. London: Hamish Hamilton, 1963.

Wall, Richard, and Jay Winter, eds. *The Upheaval of War*. Cambridge: Cambridge University Press, 1988.
Wiltsher, Anne. *Most Dangerous Women: Feminist Peace Campaigners of the Great War*. London: Pandora, 1985.

Literary Criticism

Aichinger, Peter. *The American Soldier in Fiction, 1880–1963: A History of Attitudes towards Warfare and the Military Establishment*. Ames: Iowa State University Press, 1975.
Beauman, Nicola. *A Very Great Profession: The Woman's Novel, 1914–39*. London: Virago Press, 1983.
Bergonzi, Bernard. *Heroes' Twilight: A Study of the Literature of the Great War*. London: Constable and Co., 1965.
Cooper, Helen M., Adrienne Auslander Munich, and Susan Merrill Squier, eds. *Arms and the Women: War, Gender, and Literary Representation*. Chapel Hill and London: University of North Carolina Press, 1989.
Duplessis, Rachel Blau. "Feminist Narrative in Virginia Woolf." *Novel* 21.
Fussell, Paul. *The Great War and Modern Memory*. Oxford: Oxford University Press, 1975.
Gilbert, Sandra M. "Soldier's Heart: Literary Men, Literary Women, and the Great War." *Signs* 8, no. 3 (Spring 1983).
———, and Susan Gubar. *The Madwoman in the Attic: The Woman Writer and the Nineteenth-Century Literary Imagination*. New Haven: Yale University Press, 1979.
Goldman D., ed. *Women and World War I: The Written Response*. London: Macmillan, 1993.
Johnstone, J. K. "World War I and the Novels of Virginia Woolf." In *Promise of Greatness*, edited by G. A. Panichas. London: Cassell, 1968.
Jones, Nora, and Liz Ward, eds. *The Forgotten Army: Women's Poetry of the First World War*. Beverly, Calif.: Highgate Publications, 1991.
Khan, Nosheen. *Women's Poetry of the First World War*. Brighton: Harvester Press, 1988.
Klein, Holger, ed. *The First World War in Fiction*, London: Macmillan, 1976.
Murdoch, Brian. "*Hinter Die Kulissen Des Krieges Sehen:* Adrienne Thomas, Evadne Price—and E. M. Remarke." *Forum for Modern Language Studies* 28, no. 1 (1992).
Ouditt, Sharon. *Fighting Forces, Writing Women: Identity and Ideology in the First World War*. London and New York: Routledge, 1994.
Parfitt, George. *Fiction of the First World War: A Study*. Faber and Faber, London, 1988.
Sensibar, Judith. " 'Behind the Lines' in Edith Wharton's *A Son at the Front:* Rewriting a Masculinist Tradition." *Journal of American Studies* 24, no. 2 (1990).
Showalter, Elaine. *The Female Malady: Women, Madness, and English Culture, 1830–1980*. New York: Pantheon; London: Virago, 1987.
Tomlinson, H. M. "War Books." *Criterion* 36 (1930).

Tylee, Claire M. *The Great War and Women's Consciousness: Images of Militarism and Womanhood in Women's Writings, 1914–1964*. London: Macmillan, 1990.

————. "Maleness Run Riot: The Great War and Women's Resistance to Militarism." *Women's Studies International Forum* 2, no. 3 (1988).

INDEX

149

THE AUTHORS

Dorothy Goldman is director of the School of Continuing Education at the University of Kent at Canterbury. She holds a B.A. and an M.A. from Manchester University and a Ph.D. from Keele University. She is the author of introductions to Dorothy Canfield's novels *Her Son's Wife* and *The Brimming Cup* and to Wilkie Collins's *Basil*, and editor of the essay collection *Women and World War I: The Written Response*.

Jane Gledhill is a part-time lecturer for the English and Theology Boards at the University of Kent. She holds a B.A. from York University and an M.Litt. and a Ph.D. from Keele University. Her publications include an essay on H. D. (Hilda Doolittle) and Rebecca West in *Women and World War I: The Written Response*.

Judith Anne Hattaway is access coordinator at the University of Kent at Canterbury, where she also lectures in English. She holds a B.A. and an M.A. from the University of New Zealand. Her essay on Virginia Woolf appears in *Women and World War I: The Written Response*. She has been a contributor to the journals *Wasafiri* and *English Language Notes*.